CREATING A
LIFE
FROM THE
ASHES

A MEMOIR

FIDELE SEBAHIZI, Ph.D.

ISBN: 979-8-89316-853-2 (paperback)
ISBN: 979-8-89316-854-9 (hardcover)
ISBN: 979-8-89316-852-5 (eBook)

GET YOUR FREE GIFT

To get the best experience with this book, I've
found readers who download and use
***Creating a Life from the Ashes* Companion
Reflections Worksheet**
are able to more quickly integrate the lessons
in their own life and take the next steps
in achieving their own American dream.

You can get your copy by visiting:
www.creatingalifefromtheashes.com

This book is dedicated to
the Sebahizi genealogy

TABLE OF CONTENTS

INTRODUCTION

Many people struggle to find genuine inspiration. Unfortunately, they linger over the unnecessary, wasting time and missing their potential for success. This applies to the rich and the poor. However, those surrounded by unlimited opportunities unconsciously underestimate the potential they have to excel.

In this book, I am going to show you how, as an immigrant from a poor and undeveloped village in the eastern Democratic Republic of Congo in Africa, I took advantage of American opportunities as a political refugee to overcome obstacles in my life. Looking back on my early years, from being a child in Africa to being forty-one years old in the United States, I have come a long way. My experiences should not be compared to other people's to validate their importance. What I have gone through in different countries, refugee camps, and livelihoods should be inspirational rather than judgmental. I hope to inspire you to get out of your comfort zone to better yourself. I wrote this book in an attempt to offer you my life experiences as inspirational tools. Inspiration comes from various sources. I am optimistic that how I dealt with my difficulties will encourage you to take steps toward greater achievements. Understandably, my life experiences may differ from yours. Still, you can relate to them in one way or another.

I believe in human connectedness. I enjoy listening to people's stories. Sharing my story has been a therapeutic device because it has been a relief. It's like breathing out heavily. It also makes me vulnerable. However, the more I share my life experiences, the more it gets me out of loneliness. Having people willing to listen to me makes me feel empowered, which has created freedom out of uneasy, rough memories over the years.

As an immigrant, I hope this memoir will be beneficial to fellow immigrants worldwide. Immigrants across the globe experience similar situations in host countries. Unfortunately, I have learned that many immigrants get stuck and find themselves entangled in unfamiliar circumstances in new countries. I have also discovered that the lack of better orientation in host nations creates a major setback for immigrants. As a result, new immigrants trust and lean on resettled immigrants for advice. Regrettably, because those resettled immigrants needed better orientation themselves when they first arrived, they recommend that the new immigrants follow their paths because it's the only way they know.

I promise that my true story will inspire you even if you are not an immigrant. When I was growing up in an undeveloped African village with no roads or modern technology and surviving wars, I never knew I would be in the United States one day. After surviving an atrocious massacre in a United Nations refugee camp in Burundi—a neighboring Congolese country—I never knew I would one day be a police officer and hold a Ph.D. in the United States.

I decided to write this book to inspire immigrants and nonimmigrants by giving them reasons to strive. I promise that you won't regret reading this book.

I managed to get through disappointment and intimidation in my new country and culture. I encourage you to read and be inspired by how I overcame several obstacles, which many use as excuses for not making their dreams come true. Each chapter provides inspirational true stories that will fill you with gratitude for the rest of your life.

CHAPTER 1

BIJOMBO: MY BELOVED BIRTHPLACE

Those who wish to forget painful thoughts do well to absent themselves for a while from the ties and objects that recall them, but we can be said only to fulfill our destiny in the place that gave us birth.
– William Hazlitt

I will walk you through my childhood experiences in an undeveloped village, showing you where I was born and grew up and the conditions I experienced. It would not make a lot of sense to write about some of the critical events of my life if I failed to mention my home village and what life was like in it. When you understand the foundation of my life, what follows will be more comprehensible. Just like my children, you can understand the weight of my accomplishments only after you know about my life in my native village. The purpose is not to make my accomplishments seem worthier. My goal is to show you that there is no excuse not to achieve exceptional things, no matter your past or current circumstances.

GROWING UP IN AN UNDEVELOPED VILLAGE

One day, I told my thirteen-year-old and six-year-old American-born children about Bijombo, my birthplace and home village. I recounted how it was undeveloped. They paid extra attention to my story because it appeared they did not believe what I was telling them. I informed them that my village did not have roads, vehicles, or bicycles. Unlike houses found in cities, mine had no electricity, refrigerator, television, microwave, or other household electronics, including a telephone. Villagers used vintage lanterns at night, and only some houses were equipped with one.

"What?" my children asked. Their jaws dropped, and their eyes shrank, changing their expressions as they stared at me, unblinking. "Ooh, Daddy!" they said. One patted me on my shoulder while kissing my forehead in a sympathetic gesture to comfort me. I felt relieved by telling my unbelievable, true story. Although I was telling this to my children, I felt the need to be heard. I also wanted to ensure that my children learned about my humble early life.

In 1982, I was born in a Christian family in Bijombo, a village in a highlands region known as the Hauts Plateaux (French for "high plateaus") of the South Kivu province in the Democratic Republic of Congo. My village is about thirty miles west of Uvira, an Eastern Congolese town on the border with Burundi. It is about fifteen miles west of Bujumbura, the capital city of Burundi. (There may be other regions in Africa or the world called the Hauts Plateaux, referring to mountainous areas.)

I was born in a family of seven children—four boys and three girls. I am second to last from my mother's womb. My father was the only nurse in Bijombo and the surrounding villages until another nurse joined him. He ran a small dispensary, which served dozens of villages from different corners of the region. The sick would come day and night from surrounding villages to receive treatment from my father. Sometimes, he walked countless miles to different villages to treat people. I learned that my father received medical training at the General Hospital of Uvira in 1966. After the Simba Mulele rebellion ended in the late 1960s, when Banyamulenge families were reestablishing their villages after militias had destroyed them, community elders chose my father to go to nursing training to become their nurse in their reestablished villages.

I was born in the Banyamulenge ethnic group.

The Banyamulenge is a Congolese ethnic group (also referred to as the Tutsis of South Kivu, among other current and previous names) whose home region is the Hauts Plateaux. Like other Congolese citizens, they are found throughout the country. The Banyamulenge speak Kinyamulenge, a language close to Kinyarwanda from Rwanda and Kirundi from Burundi. Kinyamulenge is unique because it includes many words from other local Congolese languages. According to linguistic experts,[1] Kinyamulenge is recognized as a distinct dialect. Like other ethnic groups in the area, Banyamulenge ancestors came many centuries ago from different parts of the region, including Rwanda, Burundi, Tanzania, and Uganda. Historian Mutambo[2] shows that some ancestors of the Banyamulenge—for example, the descendants of Byinshi—may have left the kingdom of Rwanda between 1444 and 1477, during King Yuhi II Gahima II's reign.

---

[1] Barbara F. Grimes, "Ethnologue: Languages of the World," Summer Institute of Linguistics, Inc., Dallas, Texas, 1992.

[2] Joseph Mutambo J., *Les Banyamulenge: Qui sont-ils? D'où viennent-ils? Quel rôle ont-ils joué (et pourquoi) dans le processus de la libération du Zaïre?* (Kinshasa, Democratic Republic of the Congo: [publisher not identified], 1997).

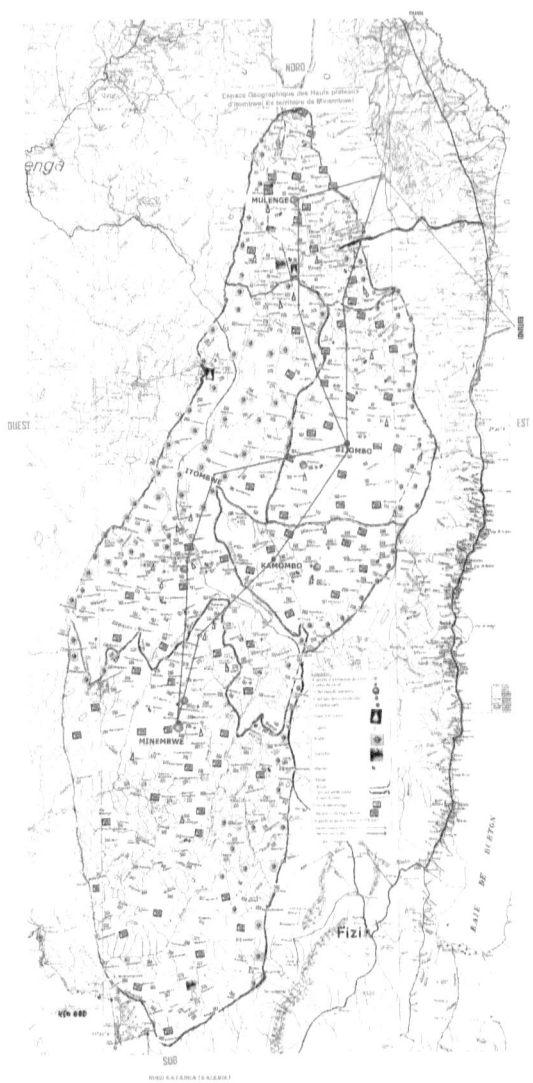

Figure 1.1: The highlands region of the South Kivu province
The map shows the major areas of the highlands region (Hauts Plateaux) of the South Kivu province in the Democratic Republic of Congo, including Kamombo, Itombwe (Mibunda), Minembwe, and Mulenge (and Rurambo).
Manassé S.

Historian Kagame[3] records Prince Byinshi, who was killed by his cousin Ruganzu II Ndoli after succeeding his father, Rwandan King Ndahiro II Cyamatare, who reigned between 1477 and 1510. Mutambo and Kagame state that Ruganzu II Ndoli attacked and conquered many regions, including from the east portion of Lake Kivu to the Rusizi River (east of the Democratic Republic of Congo), and forced the descendants of Byinshi to flee to distant regions (possibly into what became the Congolese territory after the partition of African countries' boundaries during the Berlin Conference of 1885). Kanyamachumbi[4] writes that Byinshi's descendants left the center of Rwanda around the sixteenth century. Depelchin[5] and Muzuri[6] say the Banyamulenge people arrived in the Democratic Republic of Congo before 1855. Despite living in the Congolese territory for centuries before the current national borders were set during the Berlin Conference of 1885, the Banyamulenge have faced severe discrimination, marginalization, and persecution, including accusations of being foreigners and immigrants in their own country. The country's history shows that even Belgian colonists discriminated against them by annulling[7] their autonomous, customary

---

[3] Alexis Kagame, *Un abrégé de l'ethno-histoire du Rwanda*, 1st edition (Rwanda: Éditions universitaires du Rwanda, 1972).

[4] P. Kanyamachumbi, *Société, culture et pouvoir politique en Afrique interlacustre: Hutu et Tutsi de l'ancien Rwanda* (Kinshasa: Editions Select, 1995).

[5] M. F. J. Depelchin, "From pre-capitalism to imperialism: A history of social and economic formations in Eastern Zaïre (Uvira Zone, c. 1800   1965)" (doctoral dissertation), Stanford University, 1974.

[6] Gasinzira Muzuri, "Evolution des conflits ethniques dans l'Itombwe (Sud Kivu): Des origines à l'an 1982" (doctoral dissertation), Université de Lubumbashi, 1983.

[7] Jean-Claude Willame, *Banyarwanda et Banyamulenge: Violences ethniques et gestion de l'identitaire au Kivu* (Paris, France: L'Harmattan, 1997).

administrative entities in 1933.[8] Since then, the Banyamulenge have been treated as foreigners and immigrants from Rwanda.

Discrimination against the Banyamulenge community by the general population in Uvira in 1996 was not a new practice. For example, we had heard about what the Banyamulenge experienced in Uvira in the early 1990s. We had always been considered foreigners in our country. Unfortunately, it is still the case today. In our home villages, discrimination occurred only when members of our ethnic group did not get along with other ethnic groups. Whenever it happened, members of other ethnic groups called us Banyarwanda or Rwandans (people from Rwanda), referencing that our ancestors came from what had become the Republic of Rwanda many centuries earlier. In the absence of problems, they called us Banyamulenge.

I just showed you how different and challenging it was to grow up in a disadvantaged village. Even my children found it difficult to believe where I spent my childhood. My story struck sympathy in them. I found it helpful to tell my childhood story, especially to my children, to use it as a learning tool. Reflecting on your early years is essential when it comes to evaluating your progress.

Now that you have glanced at my childhood story, I will go into detail and provide a big picture of my village—its composition, description, and housing structure.

---

[8] Filip Reyntjens et al., *Conflits au Kivu: Antecedents et enjeux* (Belgium: Universiteit Antwerpen, 1996).

THE COMPOSITION OF VILLAGES

This section will demonstrate how my village and surrounding villages were composed and socially linked to each other, although they were apart from each other.

Bijombo consisted of several small villages. There was Bijombo Center, the main village, from which the name was derived. The center was one of a few villages built in the highlands region and one of the two first villages with a church, school, and medical facility. That is where I was born and raised to the age of fourteen. Bijombo Center was built on a hill called Ku Mashuri, meaning "at school." The village was named after the first school built in it—the first in the area—indicating that the village was at school. Other villages surrounded Bijombo Center.

Banyamulenge families occupied some villages, while other ethnic communities, such as Bafulero, Babembe, and Banyindu, occupied others. It was very rare for different ethnic groups to share a village. Wherever it occurred, only a few families lived with community members who did not belong to them. Each ethnic group occupied its own village for the most part. Mostly, this was due to cultural and linguistic differences. Also, each village was on its own hill. The Banyamulenge villages included:

- Mashuri or Bijombo Center
- Mutara
- Ishenge
- Rusuku
- Bikinga (also called Nyakidegu)
- Kuwigiti

- Bijombo (a village different from Bijombo Center)
- Kuwamarumba

Villages belonging to other ethnic groups, namely Bafulero, Babembe, and Banyindu, included:

- Ishenge (Bafulero)
- Kuwigiti (Babembe)
- Kibindibindi (Bafulero)
- Murambi (Banyindu)
- Mu Baturika (Bafulero)
- Kwa Nyagahebe (Bafulero)
- Gateja (Bafulero)

All of these villages were about three to five miles from each other. Generally speaking, all of these villages were collectively named after Bijombo. For example, when someone needed to identify where they were from, they would say things like, "I am from Bijombo, Ku Mashuri," meaning they were from Bijombo Center.

Figure 1.2: Bijombo Center church before it was destroyed
This is the church of Bijombo Center (Ku Mashuri), my home village. The picture was taken before the village was destroyed during the violent ethnic conflict in the area toward the end of the 21st century's second decade.
Alexis Bahivi Rugazura

Figure 1.3: Bijombo Center after it was destroyed
The picture shows the Bijombo Center's destructive state. In October 2019, the Banyamulenge's neighboring ethnic groups destroyed the village, which is the main Bijombo village. The village was built in the circled area.
Joseph

Figure 1.4: Rusuku village before it was destroyed
The village is called Rusuku. It was one of the Bijombo villages before it was destroyed during the ethnic conflict toward the end of the 21st century's second decade. The Banyamulenge inhabitants were forced out of the village by their neighbors, turning it into a cornfield.
Alexis Bahivi Rugazura

Figure 1.5: Rusuku village after it was destroyed
The picture shows the Rusuku village's destructive state. In October 2019, the Banyamulenge's neighboring ethnic groups destroyed the village, which is one of the Bijombo's villages. The village was built in the circled area. It was turned into a cornfield.
Joseph

Nevertheless, Bijombo (see Figure 1.1) was a big name in the area. The Bijombo District villages were from dozens to hundreds of miles away from each other. There were hundreds of villages in the Bijombo District. They belonged to different ethnic communities. Some of them were:

- Kagogo
- Tchanzovu
- Kanyaga
- Mugeti
- Gahuna
- Mugogo
- Murambya
- Kiziba
- Kirumba
- Gatanga
- Maheta
- Kajembwe
- Kanono
- Gongwa
- Kanogo
- Rubibi
- Rumagaza
- Gihuha
- Kajoka
- Mitamba

There were several Protestant denominations in the area. The three prominent ones were the 37th CADC (Communauté des Assemblées de Dieu au Congo in French, or Community of Assemblies of God in Congo), the 8th CEPAC (Communauté des Eglises de Pentecôte en Afrique Centrale in French, or Community of Pentecostal Churches in Central Africa), and CLMC (Communauté Libre Méthodiste au Congo in French, or Free Methodist Community in Congo). All ethnic groups belonged to all religious denominations, although most of the time, each ethnic group had its own parish. They all had the same church leadership and frequently organized big church gatherings together, such as during Christmas, Easter, and Pentecost festivals. Each parish would bring its choir(s) to the conferences as the parish representation, meaning dozens of choirs would participate and sing at a conference.

The Bijombo District was surrounded by other major areas with hundreds of villages, including Rurambo, Kamombo, Mibunda, and Minembwe (see Figure 1.1). These five areas comprised the green highlands known as the Hauts Plateaux of the South Kivu province, also called the Hauts Plateaux of Minembwe or Mulenge. The aforementioned ethnic groups lived in other areas and villages that did not constitute the highlands of the Hauts Plateaux.

The composition of the villages suggests that such a configuration might have exacerbated ethnic disharmony and conflict, with the Banyamulenge on one side and the rest of the ethnic groups on the other. It is because other ethnic communities have always considered the Banyamulenge foreigners and immigrants even though they have been in the country for centuries. It is difficult to explain why this is still the case. However, politicians have played a significant role in dividing the population to gain more popularity. Geopolitics has, in fact, played a notable role in the discrimination the Banyamulenge have experienced from their neighbors and the country's local and central governments.

It should be highlighted that the Banyamulenge is a very small ethnic group compared to other groups (there has not been an official census to know the number of the Banyamulenge). Diversity is good for increasing productivity, innovation, knowledge, and more. But, while writing this book, I understood that all ethnic groups in our villages ignored the benefits diversity brings because ethnic conflict remains volatile today. Hundreds of Banyamulenge villages have been burned to ashes. The former villages have been turned into fields for cultivating corn, beans, and other crops.

Understanding the significance of cultural diversity enables us to be aware of possible causes of ethnic conflict.

Considering the village composition, I will introduce how villages were built to create a big picture of my village.

THE DESCRIPTION OF VILLAGES

Villages were different in size. Some were bigger and more populated than others. Some were named after individuals, especially the first person who occupied the village or an influential person in the village. Most villages—specifically, preeminent ones—comprised several hut houses and a church.

One family would have a couple of houses, including the main house, which was considered a kitchen (or *igitekero* in Kinyamulenge), a parents' house, and sometimes a small house for teenagers. (Unless otherwise specified, all words throughout the book that are not English will be in Kinyamulenge and in italics, except names and places.) The *igitekero* was not simply a cooking kitchen but a common area where the whole family sat, talked, and ate before bed. This house had a central fireplace for cooking and grilling food for the entire family.

A church building was distinguished from others because it was the only building in most villages with a sheet metal roof. The rest of the houses had grass roofs. The church walls were made of bricks, while the walls of regular huts were mainly made of bamboo. In addition to the church building, two other buildings, *urubunga* and *amaombi*, were dedicated to prayers and church-related activities, such as a choir rehearsal. These two structures were built with grass roofs, like other houses in the village. The *urubunga* was used to welcome church guests in the village, while the *amaombi* was used for long-term prayers called *ihuduma*.

Figure 1.6: One of the village settings
This is a village setting in my home region, showing the type of houses (painted in white) I was born and raised in and small building structures for domestic animals.
Unknown

Figure 1.7: A village on a hill
Villages were built on hills covered by trees with no roads.
Gedeon

Besides families' houses and the church, a village contained tiny buildings for domestic animals, primarily calves, goats, sheep, and chickens. Toilets and spaces for bathing were outside the houses. They were small and neglected structures that appeared insignificant in villagers' lives.

Most of these small buildings were in wreckage, most of the time lacking doors, windows, and roofs. Pieces of clothing served as doors. Some people took showers in buckets standing on their bed frames inside their houses. They removed the mattress, took a bath while standing on the bed frame, and returned the mattress after showering. Some families possessed structures where they stored food products, such as potatoes, beans, and corn. A village with a clinic and a school—for instance, my home village, Bijombo Center—would be a few miles from other villages. Small footpaths linked houses, buildings, and other structures within a village.

Although they were away from the villages, small sources of running water existed in the valleys between hills and villages. Villagers went to them to fetch water for drinking and showering. They did laundry in larger streams in the valley, creating a back-and-forth friction movement between both hands. The friction was done repeatedly until the clothes were clean and ready to be rinsed. One of the methods to rinse clothes was twisting them until little to no water was left. Then the clothes would be laid down to dry in grass or on small bushes.

Families with cows built small structures on separate hills where they kept and milked them. Each family also had its place for farming. Farming fields were divided based on the crops of the season. There were extensive fields for corn, potatoes, beans, etc.

Villagers also built a flea market on its own hill, away from villages. One market served dozens of villages in one area. The market operated only once a week. For example, in Bijombo Center, the flea market called Mu Gatanu (*gatanu* means "five") opened only on Fridays. Villages had no convenience stores. Unlike in the United States, where buying something from Walmart takes minutes, if a villager forgot to buy something on market day, they had to wait for the following week or go to another market very far away from their own village. However, some villages contained a few merchants who stored some products in their houses, waiting for the next market day. These home-based merchants sold their products between market days.

This description shows how my village setting differed from neighborhoods in any given city. It was not an easy life, especially when I think about it now. After living in the United States for many years, I have learned that many people fail to realize how affluent they are compared to the people of my childhood. My childhood has never left me, so when I run into such people, I think back and judge them for not knowing what a rough life looks and feels like. On the other hand, when I was growing up, I did not know how different my childhood was because it was all I knew.

Having different perspectives on life will help you appreciate what you possess. As a result, peace will overflow your heart.

In the next section, I will narrow my description to the housing structure, providing a concrete understanding of the life I experienced in my childhood.

HOUSING STRUCTURE

Unlike fancy and strong structures in a city, the houses in my village were not stable. That is because most buildings, especially dwelling structures, had no foundation. They lacked modern, sophisticated architecture. Though the houses lasted for many years, they remained basic in convenience and comfort.

The typical house consisted of wood, soil, and grass materials. The majority were in the form of a perfect circle. These huts did not need a foundation. A flat surface was enough for inserting sharpened wood, mainly bamboo, into the ground for the wall. Bamboo was also preferred for the roof. Bamboo was convenient as it did not require great skills or tools to split it in half.

Figure 1.8: Sharpening wood
Sharpening wood for construction was men's responsibility. Some trees could not be sharpened. Therefore, these were not suitable for construction.
Alexis Bahivi Rugazura

The wall structure was a combination of vertical and horizontal pieces of wood. A rope linked the pieces of wood together. The homeowner used wiring and knots to ensure the horizontal pieces of wood did not slide to the ground. After this step, the wall looked like it was made of several small squares. Then, a mixture of dirt, cow poop, and water was inserted to fill up the empty squares. Cow poop was preferred and was thought to sustain the mix well. Soil and water alone did not make a sustainable mixture.

The roof structure was built on the ground. After its completion, the homeowner requested assistance from able-bodied male adults in the village or surrounding villages to lift the roof and place it on the top of the wall, an activity the villagers referred to as *guterura igisenge* ("lifting the roof"). Then grass would be meticulously put on top of the roof, which was called *gusakara*. The *gusakara* activity resulted in grasses' heads and tails overlapping. Not all villagers knew how to perform this activity; people sometimes requested assistance from village experts.

Figure 1.9: The construction of a house roof in the village
The house roof was built upside down inside the wall frame to ensure it would fit during repositioning. After constructing the roof in this position, villagers would lift it out of the wall frame and place it on top of the wall in the pyramid position.
Unknown

Most huts had at least one bedroom. The rooms' interior walls were built with the same materials as the outside walls. Some doors were wood with metal locking mechanisms. Others were made of intertwined wooden materials and had no locking mechanisms. This door type was not attached to the doorframe like regular doors. The only method to close it was to slide it through two wooden poles fixed on each side of the frame. Elderly people mostly used this door type.

Except for the church and a few exceptional houses, the rest of the houses in the village had a circular hole in the outside kitchen and bedroom walls. The holes had no glass to cover them. Instead, villagers used pieces of clothing to fill them in. That was all it took. There were no other windows.

The typical house's floor was dirt, and villagers laid grass on it. Some floors had grass and a mat made of grass on the top. No tiles were available for house or church floors, walls, or roofs. (There was also no grass on the church's floor.)

A house had two spaces for storing firewood. One (*urusenge*) was right above the fireplace. Most houses had a wooden bar for chickens under this storage and on the other side of the fireplace by the wall. The second storage (*idari*) was in the opposite direction, across from the *urusenge*. This *idari* storage was also the bedroom ceiling because it was right above the bed. Most of the time, dishes and other household items were located by the wall between the two firewood storage spaces.

Figure 1.10: Firewood storage
Urusenge, the firewood storage was built right above the fireplace.
Gedeon

Village painting styles were fascinating and served an aesthetic purpose. When it was time to paint or repaint a house, villagers utilized different soil colors, including red, yellow, white, black, gray, and mixtures of any of the colors. Any mix needed cow poop for mixture sustainability. On the outside wall, two colors usually sufficed. The bottom section was always shorter than the top. Most painting designs appeared on the inside wall, especially by the fireplace. Women and girls did the job because it was assumed to be their responsibility. They drew several geometrical and other shapes, including circles, triangles, squares, rectangles, parallelograms, polygons, stars, and hearts.

Figure 1.11: Painting houses, a women's responsibility
Painting was considered a women's activity. They used various colors to paint on the outside and inside walls.
Unknown

My experience growing up in such housing should be a lesson for being grateful for what you have or the type of housing structure you reside in. Looking back on my childhood, I know that this way of life is still the case today for those who live in my home region. I wish I had the means to develop such primitive villages to allow villagers to experience a better life.

Have you ever complained about what you have, such as your house or older (or newer) car? After reading my story, does it relate to yours? Should you be more grateful?

Now, with the housing structure in mind, I will explain what it was like to be a child in an undeveloped village.

TOYS AND SCHOOL PUNISHMENTS FEW KNOW EXIST

It is easier to imagine another person's life if you have experienced it or a similar one. In this short section, I will describe the toys I played with and how different they were from what you might have played with in childhood. In my village, girls and boys did not have a variety of toys to play with. One difference between my childhood and the childhoods of most of this book's readers is that parents in my village did not have to buy their children's toys. But kids were innovative enough to make their own toys without their parents' help.

Like in other places around the world, boys and girls had different activities, often playing games that imitated what they would do in adulthood. The village had no modern toys seen in developed countries. Boys, for instance, cut small tree branches in a V shape that resembled cow horns because boys and men were responsible for raising and looking after cattle. Then, they bumped the tree horns into each other, pretending the tree cows were fighting. The horns were in different sizes, indicating different sizes and types of cows, including bulls and calves. Boys also played dangerous games, such as swinging on ropes naturally attached to trees without knowing how tight the ropes were. Swinging on a rope hanging from a tree on a steep hill would throw a boy in the valley if the rope detached from the tree.

Figure 1.12: Tree cows, boys' preferred toys
Little boys made and played with V-shaped tree branches resembling cow horns.
David

On the other hand, girls played with corn cobs (*imitiritiri*), dressing them in clothing and calling them babies, imitating a woman's role of raising and caring for her baby. They put the cobs on their backs and covered them with a traditional loincloth (*urupande*), which resembled the way adult women carried a human baby. They also played grinding crops. They would place broken pieces of corn in a small container, such as an empty medication bottle, and attempt to crush them with a small piece of wood, copying what their mothers and older sisters did with actual grinding.

I began first grade in my home village of Bijombo Center. The school system had no pre-kindergarten or kindergarten program. The first grade was the starting point for all children. Unlike in the United States, there was no standardized age requirement for starting school. Though age played a small role in enrolling children in specific grades, older children were embarrassed to study with younger ones in the same class.

My primary school served four or five villages. One class contained about twenty children. Unlike in the United States or other developed countries, there were no government or other requirements or penalties for parents who did not enroll their children in school. Attending school was only a parental decision. Children studied several subjects, including French, mathematics, religion, music, and sports.

The school system punished children to ensure they learned and understood correctly. Unlike in the United States, where the school records a student's tardiness on a progress report, students at my elementary school received physical punishment for being late. Punishment involved striking the student's palms or legs with a stick, causing visible bruising. Another punishment was demanding that the student bring something from home to school or the teacher, such as a homemade grass broom. This kind of punishment required the involvement of the student's parents. They had to make or buy a broom to respond to the school's or teacher's demands.

Every morning, all students lined up and sang the national anthem and other motivational songs before entering classrooms for instruction. Students who walked while singing the anthem were punished because it was considered disobedient to the country and its flag. Students who failed to line up outside for the anthem were also punished. Those who came to school while the national anthem was being sung or after it was sung were punished for being late.

You can see how disadvantaged I was as a child and how I needed better and various educational toys and disciplinary actions that were not hateful or physically harsh.

If you are reading this book and have not experienced what I experienced, you should be glad you did not. If you are an immigrant like me and went through similar experiences, it is worth looking back and enjoying what you have now and how your children, if you have them, are cared for at school.

In the next section, I will introduce you to village and church activities so you can understand how villagers generally lived. These activities were dear to them.

Figure 1.13: School structures
Most schools were poorly built and had impoverished equipment. It rained on students during class sessions.
Gedeon

FASCINATING VILLAGE ACTIVITIES

The lives of villagers were busy every day with numerous activities, such as agricultural and church duties. It was apparent that women had many more physically demanding tasks than men. They were also busier than men. For instance, they were responsible for gathering firewood, fetching household water from a water source in valleys, and grinding corn grain for flour, which took days to complete. Even when a village expected a church conference, women were responsible for painting houses, gathering and storing dry firewood, and doing other strenuous activities.

Men did some hard work as well. They were in charge of caring for cows and part of the farming (getting the land ready by removing trees and bushes), to name a few responsibilities. During the summer, when the grass was dry, men and boys took cows far away from the village (*gusuhura*) for green pasture. They walked hundreds of miles with a herd of cattle, looking for non-dry grass (*mu biraro*). They stayed in the area for months and returned in the fall, when the grass was green again at home.

My uncle, Muhaya, and I took his cows to a location called Mu Rukuri, a grazing place in the Mibunda area, some forty-five miles west of my village, Bijombo Center. I was in my early teens, and the place was bushy and scary. Whenever my uncle sent me alone to watch cows grazing or drinking water, I was frightened, worrying that wild animals would attack me. At night, we slept in a small handmade grassy structure. The building had no doors or windows. The walls were made of small tree branches and grass. We could see cows outside from inside. We slept on a small cowskin (*uruhu or igikubo*). The skin was dry and partially covered the grassy sleeping area, which was beside a fireplace. We moved to different places during our time there, destroying and building temporary grassy structures each time. We spent about two months in those woods.

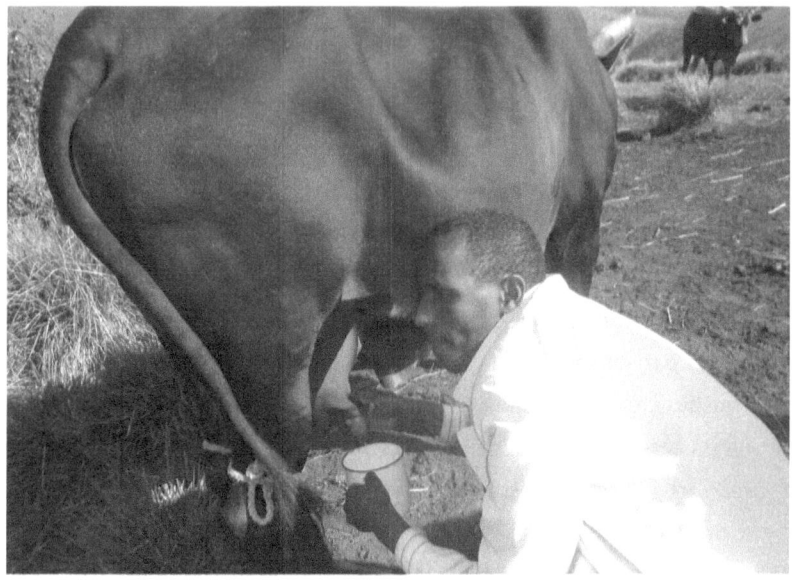

Figure 1.14: A man milking a cow
Men and boys were also charged with milking cows for women, children, and the entire family.
Alexis Bahivi Rugazura

Regarding growing food, men did the part of the farming that pertained to preparing for it. They focused on building fences around the field to prevent animals from ruining the crops. They also prepared the field for planting seeds. If a field had bushes or trees, it was men's job to remove them. Then, women grew food by planting seeds and periodically removing weeds from the crops (*kubagara*) until harvest. Women and girls spent most of their time grinding seeds for food (*guhura*). Making flour took a long time. Women and girls were also responsible for fetching water (*kuvoma*) from water sources, gathering firewood (*gutoragura*) from bushes, and doing laundry (*kumesa*) with their hands at a river.

Figure 1.15: Girls heading to the river to wash clothes
Girls and women carried dirty clothes and walked to the river to hand wash all family's clothes. Sometimes, some men washed their own clothes, but the activity was considered women's.
Unknown

Figure 1.16: Women washing clothes at the river
Washing clothes was considered women's responsibility, and it was primarily done away from the village at a river or small water source.
Unknown

Villagers stood in solidarity with one another. Solidarity was very significant to their survival. It was like an implied law, a social contract that everyone obeyed. For instance, preparing a field for farming was a tough job that required many hands. The farm owner requested assistance from the rest of the men in the village. Dozens of them delightedly answered the call for help free of charge. They gathered in the field to be worked on with their machetes and other farming tools in what was known as *umurari* (the gathering of able-bodied men to perform a job as a group). For drinkers, the farm owner bought a traditional homemade alcoholic corn beverage (*umumera*) to enjoy during and after the task. For nondrinkers, the owner found something else, such as fresh corn to grill and share during and after work.

Church choirs also engaged in this type of solidarity to fund their activities. They worked together for a cause. They found someone who needed help, for instance, farming. Then they assisted them and received payment. They worked as a group to get the job done quickly. Because Christianity played a vital role in villagers' lives, drinking alcoholic beverages was considered a sin and was done by only a few. Teenage boys and male adults enjoyed drinking the *umumera* because it contained little to no alcohol. Many drank it for fun. However, it was considered taboo for a girl or a woman to drink.

As you finish reading these paragraphs, I hope you understand that, like in many other cultures worldwide, women and girls in my culture carried a heavy burden in keeping village life running. They were the backbone of families, not just by giving birth to and raising children but by engaging every day in physically demanding tasks. After all, solidarity among villagers was a lifesaver and enabled them to work together to accomplish what a single person could not.

Though I had a tough life growing up, I cherish my culture. But at the same time, I think some things should have been changed for the better.

You can learn from this that my humble beginnings did not dictate my future. If you face life challenges, such as poverty, take heart and believe your future will be bright.

CHURCH LIFE IN BIJOMBO AND SURROUNDING VILLAGES

Villagers practiced Christianity in multiple forms. I will discuss and describe three unique and distinguished ways villagers worshipped God: church conferences (*umukutano*), prayer trips (*umusitari*), and prayer and fasting (*ihuduma*).

Church conferences occurred a couple of times a year. Permanent annual conferences were Christmas, Easter, and Pentecost. There were also periodic gatherings that churches organized from time to time. A denomination district picked a village to host a conference for the year. A district had several hundred villages. All the villages gathered in the chosen village for the conference. The gathering lasted at least three days: Friday, Saturday, and Sunday. But some people, especially those dedicated to consistent, intense prayers, went one or two days earlier to prepare spiritually for the conference. Sometimes, each village would bring its contribution (food or money) to the conference. However, the host village was expected to provide everything free of charge, including food, places for guests to sleep, and other necessities. Villagers who hosted the conference carried the heaviest burden, including women and girls having to paint their houses (*guhoma*) in preparation for the conference. It was customary for host villagers to give up their bedrooms for guests. For example, a married woman would give up her bed so a male guest could sleep with her husband.

Prayer trips were enjoyable. A group of prayer members would depart from their villages for a prayer journey, going to one village after another, spending weeks, sometimes months, praying for several requests for themselves and others. Host villages were responsible for providing food, a place to sleep, and other necessities. Sometimes, prayer members on these trips did not have to announce their arrival in a village. Regardless of how they arrived in a village, announced or unannounced, host villagers provided everything needed for the guests. Sometimes, these trips were combined with fasting. Prayer partners would fast for a day or two during their prayer journey. They preferred to enter a village during evening hours, when most villagers were home from their daily activities. To make this happen, they would sometimes sit and wait at a location far away from the village and enter it only when it was dark. The villagers welcomed them at the village entrance by carrying their belongings, including their walking sticks, to a guest house. Then the hosts and visitors would have a short welcoming church service (*kwiyegereza abashitsi*) and take a meal break. The main service followed the meal. A third service (*igitaramo*) for able-bodied and energetic men and women followed and lasted for the rest of the night.

The villagers occasionally conducted routine prayer and fasting services (*ihuduma*) in the village. From time to time, people from surrounding villages would come together for such a service. A group of individuals, especially those who knew each other from praying together every time, organized a prayer and fasting session for days or weeks. They preferred to isolate themselves in a prayer house, using the *urubunga* or *amaombi*, the two buildings dedicated and associated with the village's church. They allowed the general population to join them for only a short period because they wanted to be by themselves most of the time. These special sessions were conducted for a specific reason, so only those who shared and understood the burden of the prayer request(s) agreed to pray. Sometimes, the prayer request(s) remained a secret. Groups that organized prayer and fasting sessions included the church, women, youth, choir, and other random groups. Frequently, these prayer meetings occurred in a private, remote area away from the village, such as in the bush or in a cave (*ubutayu*).

Now, I will shift my storytelling to a romantic relationship.

A CULTURE THAT DIDN'T RECOGNIZE THE BOYFRIEND-GIRLFRIEND RELATIONSHIP

Not all village activities were physically demanding or painful. Others were eventful, and all the villagers enjoyed attending. Many readers may find marriage practice in my culture (at least during and before my childhood) unfit in their worlds. For example, the boyfriend-girlfriend relationship was a new concept introduced to me shortly after I left my village and found myself in a different culture. Although this has nothing to do with marriage, it is essential to consider because, in my original culture, the boyfriend-girlfriend relationship would be regarded a cultural abomination. I say "original culture" because cultures change over time, depending on several factors, including assimilation with other cultures.

Marriage practices differed depending on the culture. Various ethnic groups with distinct cultures inhabited my region. I will only discuss the marriage practice in my culture.

The modern boyfriend-girlfriend practice did not exist in our region for any of the cultures. A girl or boy began discussing personal friendship when ready to marry. People in my culture married at a very young age—for instance, fourteen years old. It was (and still is) a common practice across the board in all cultures in the area. Legally, the assumption was that it was illegal to marry while underage, especially for adult males to marry female minors. But the presumed law never worked. I never saw any male arrested or prosecuted for marrying an underage girl. Unfortunately, this is still the case today as I am writing this book.

A boy's parents went to a girl's household to ask her parents to give their daughter to their son into marriage. Sometimes, this step happened even before the boy met the girl and agreed to marry. The marriage arrangement was a deal between the parents. Other times, this phase occurred after the boy and girl agreed to marry. It happened on a case-by-case basis. Both ways worked perfectly.

Our culture allows marriage between cousins, but only between the children of a brother and a sister. Cousins whose fathers are brothers are not permitted to marry each other. Likewise, cousins whose mothers are sisters are not allowed to marry. Therefore, even today, a father prefers to go to his sister, and a mother prefers to go to her brother to ask for a bride. The parents would go to another family if no sibling had a girl ready for marriage. Sometimes, if a boy was still a child or not prepared to marry, his parent would ask the father's sister or the mother's brother to hold a marriageable girl for their son. The parent requesting a bride would provide a cow as a bride holder, or marriage in advance (*gufata irembo*). The girl then would be considered to belong to the boy's family even before marriage. The girl's family would keep and raise the cow until the girl was ready for marriage, and the cow and its offspring would be part of the girl's dowry, adding more cows for the full dowry.

When approaching marriage, family members from both families, as well as designated villagers, discussed and agreed on how many cows the boy's family would give the girl's family for the dowry (*inkwano* or *gukoshanya*). Only men participated (and still participate) in this cultural matter. Women were only informed of the agreement. On the marriage day, no matter how far the girl lived from the boy, dozens of villagers volunteered to walk with her to her marriage (*gucura*). The girl would weep constantly over leaving her siblings, parents, and friends behind.

Upon entering the boy's village, people would meet the girl's companions at the village entrance singing welcoming hymns, usually religious songs (*gutega umugeni*). The girl's group picked two or three girls or women to cover the bride with a wraparound cloth worn by girls and women. The girl's group would choose a different song and sing it simultaneously with the boy's village. They sang two songs at the same time, standing still while facing each other. The villagers would help the girl's companions carry their belongings and walking sticks. Then the girl's group would give up their song and join the boy's group, everyone now singing one song. The hosts would turn around and lead the girl's cohorts into the village.

After the marriage ceremony (the church service), youths from the boy's and girl's groups performed a special dance (*ikigamba*), which lasted the entire night as they said their farewells to the girl through various songs and dances in circles. A traditional alcoholic beverage (*umumera*) would be served. The bride and bridegroom would not be present for these dances, and most parents did not partake in this after-party event.

The marriage practice in my culture might have surprised and been new to you. Learning about other people's cultures is important when it comes to connecting with or relating to each other. How does your culture differ from mine regarding marriage practice? Are there any differences? Are there any similarities?

I will now tell the story of the most painful practice I have ever experienced in my life: circumcision without anesthesia.

BRUTAL CIRCUMCISION IN THE BUSH WITHOUT ANESTHETIC

I still can't believe how I was circumcised. It feels like a dream. Neither my father nor my mother witnessed this life-threatening event, although I am sure they were aware of it. However, once in a while, I doubt they even consented to it. I never asked them. My family was not with me when it was done. You may find it difficult to believe this story. I assure you that it is not a fictional story. It was the most brutal experience I have ever gone through in my entire life up to this point.

Male circumcision was an exciting event in the village. Unlike in developed countries, circumcision did not occur at or within a few weeks after birth. It happened when children were somewhere between two and ten years old—or older, in exceptional circumstances. Waiting until this age depended on parents' or personal preferences, as there was no standardized rule to follow. This horrific type of surgery, as far as my experience is concerned, took place even in the bush. Yes, I was circumcised in the grass on the outskirts of a bush. At that time, we had two nurses in my village, one of whom was my father. The other nurse was the go-to nurse for circumcision. He was a military veteran. He circumcised me. He performed surgeries on about ten kids that day with no anesthetic drugs. He grabbed the skin and cut it with scissors. Then he sewed the broken skin with stitches. I doubt he wore gloves.

Boys had no choice but to be forced into this painful surgical procedure, and the pain lasted for weeks. Young adult men in the village divided themselves up to catch the boys ready for the surgery. They gave each other assignments regarding who would go after which boy and take them to the site for the procedure. The boys' parents were out of the game. They probably consented to the practice but never witnessed the brutal surgical procedure performed on their children. Culturally, children belonged to the village in the sense that when, for example, a child misbehaved or made a mistake, the child's parents would not complain if a random person in the village disciplined their child. That is how random youngsters in the village, excited about the task, charged themselves with taking boys, one at a time, to get butchered. It was apparent they had experienced the same hard-to-believe event when they were children. Because of how excited they seemed, it would not be an exaggeration to think they wanted other boys to feel what they had felt.

Though mine was done when I was very young, I still remember the person who caught me and took me to the circumcision location on the outskirts of the bush. That day, I learned the bad news that I was going to go through the circumcision. I overheard people talking about it, and I knew it was my day. I wanted to escape the village, but it was too late.

I do not remember how old I was when this happened. The young man (I will call him Richard) was possibly ten years older than me and surprised me. He grabbed me out of my house, and I had no choice. I began kicking him, screaming, and pulling away. But he pulled me forcibly out of the house. No family member intervened. He must have known that I had learned about the bad day. He stayed very close to me. Though I could not outrun him, it seemed that he did not want to take the chance of having to chase me around. He guided me outside the village toward the water source where we fetched drinking water.

The nurse had begun the surgery on one child while the rest were waiting their turn. Richard played with me to kill time. We were on a steep mountain right outside the village. The circumcision was taking place down the hill about a quarter mile from us.

"Do you want me to let you go?" he asked.

"Yes," I immediately answered, as if I'd known what he was going to ask me. "Please let me go. I will give you everything you want." I had nothing in mind to offer, but I thought my begging would impress him. It did not.

"Go," he said.

He let me run away from him for a few seconds before he reached out and grabbed my shirt. I do not think he did it because he believed I would give him everything he wanted. I think he did it because he just wanted to play. My friends were in front of me in the queue, but I could not hear them scream because I could not see the location where the surgery was occurring. But I did know which direction it was in.

Richard started taking me down the hill to the outskirts of the bush, where the surgery was taking place, and I knew my turn was up. I attempted to pull away from him again and kicked him, but he grabbed both of my hands and dragged me down the hill. He then put me on his shoulders and carried me down when I persisted in resisting him. I still remember what the nurse's face looked like as he was holding surgical scissors, eagerly waiting for my arrival.

Richard began taking my shorts off before we reached the nurse. He could not wait any longer. I was like a goat taken to a slaughterer. No sign of mercy was shown at all from Richard and the nurse. The nurse laid me on the grass. Nothing was between my skin and the grass. I do not remember if the nurse was wearing gloves. At least three young male adults held me down by my legs and hands while the nurse performed the surgery with scissors. I can still feel the first cut. I screamed like a pig being slaughtered to the point of losing my voice by the end of the surgery. They controlled my body and movements but were unable to control my mouth. That is all I had left to practice my freedom. I screamed for my mother's help, but she was nowhere to be found in the area.

The nurse performed surgery with no anesthetic medication. I saw the entire procedure and yelled for help without end because of the enormous pain. My blood covered me and the whole grass area. I am sure it also covered the nurse and those who were holding me down.

After the procedure, Richard took me back to the village to my mother, with me walking like a spider, with my legs and hands spread out. My mother wrapped me in a blanket, ensuring the blanket did not touch the wound. It was a couple of days before the gauze was changed. Changing the gauze was another killer. The village's young adults took turns changing gauze for all the children. They tended to do it early in the morning. We sat in warm water to let the gauze loosen before being removed. Traditional medication, such as the ashes and leaves of trees, was used to treat our wounds. Treatment also involved modern medicines but to a lesser degree.

Remembering such a painful event makes me humble, especially because there are many children worldwide who still experience this type of circumcision. For instance, Bijombo and surrounding villages have not developed since I last visited it in the early 2000s. In fact, things have been worse precisely because of the unending ethnic-motivated conflict.

You can be glad if you did not experience such a cold-blooded surgical procedure. If you did, I am sorry because I know what it feels like. Can you think of one or two things you are glad you did not experience? Have you experienced severe pain but are thankful you did not die?

In the following section, I will walk you through what I experienced with legal and governmental matters.

LEGALIZED ROBBERY THAT SOLVED "CRIMES"

It is common sense that the security forces' job is to serve and protect the general population. Unfortunately, this was not the case in the Democratic Republic of Congo. Security forces, especially soldiers, harassed and robbed people regularly. Regrettably, they abused their authority. Soldiers regarded themselves as superior even to police officers. Police officers appeared weak, intimidated, and frightened in front of the military. I recently spoke with a Congolese military commander now serving in the Congo's national army about how police officers in the United States have the power, for instance, to stop a car driven by a soldier and investigate a traffic violation. The commander laughed out loud on the other end of the telephone. "What? Police stopping a soldier?"

I learned about and witnessed the military's abuse of citizens at a very young age. The national army deployed soldiers, who had their camps outside our villages. There was no police force in our region. There was no order. Each soldier did their own things to illegally acquire money and other properties from villagers without consequences. Soldiers were disorganized, uncontrolled, and corrupt.

They even had helpers (*kaderi*), civilians, who assisted them in catching people they wanted to rob (*kunyaga*). It was a well-orchestrated system that always worked. Soldiers and their assistants entered a village and began capturing goats and chickens for themselves without the owners' consent. When villagers attempted to complain, they were beaten with wooden sticks and military cords with no mercy. Then soldiers ordered them to carry the plundered domestic animals that used to be theirs for a very long distance. There was no place to file complaints against the soldiers. They did whatever they wanted every time.

One day, cattle merchants gathered at a market in our village. The flea market had closed, and the merchants had gathered to chat before leaving. A soldier who had hidden his AK-47 and was not wearing a uniform surprised them. He appeared out of nowhere without them realizing it, and it was too late for the merchants to get away. They froze and remained seated, not knowing what to do. The soldier demanded money, but the merchants hesitated to obey. The soldier cocked his firearm and put it on his right shoulder, pointing it upward. The merchants continued hesitating because the soldier belonged to their ethnic community. They did not think he would do this to them. Ethnic belongingness was vital in villagers' lives and throughout the country (it still is), encouraging in-group favoritism. Both ordinary people and people in power expected particular treatment from members of their ethnic group. When the merchants still hesitated to obey the soldier's order, he discharged his weapon upward, firing a couple of rounds. I was there, watching with my friends. The merchants immediately reached into their bags and made a pile of bills on the grass for the soldier. The soldier grabbed the bills and left the merchants there in terror after robbing them.

Villagers were used to this military misconduct. It was a normal way of life. Even when they did not rob people, soldiers forced villagers to carry their belongings from one village to another and sometimes for a very long way—even hundreds of miles. Village peasants took turns carrying soldiers' bundles of property. Occasionally, they would be stopped on their way home from carrying soldiers' bundles to carry again for another group of soldiers. There was no negotiation, no argument.

One day, a merchant died in our house. It was customary for traveling merchants to find places to spend a night after concluding their transactions in a flea market before they continued their trip to other markets in other villages the following morning. They would spend the night at one place, going to their friends' houses after the flea market. They did not have to pay for their stays. From time to time, they did not even pay for the food they ate at the residence where they were being accommodated for the night. Most often, villagers and merchants exchanged goods (for example, food for soap). Otherwise, the villagers gave them almost everything for free. The merchant who died at our house became sick with malaria after leaving the market in the evening. He could not wake up the following morning to continue with others on their journey. He spent a couple of days at our house being treated by my father, who was still a nurse. Unfortunately, the merchant did not make it. He passed away.

A soldier stationed dozens of miles west of my village (in Kipupu) received news of the merchant's death. I do not know how he received the information because villages did not have telephone systems or other technological communications. People from my village or the surrounding villages must have informed him. He walked dozens of miles from Kipupu to Bijombo Center by himself. His presumed moral and legal reason for being there was to conduct a death investigation. However, he strayed from his official task and accused my father of killing the merchant. He intimidated him and demanded money—this was the actual reason he had walked dozens of miles. He did not conduct a death investigation. I do not think he had the knowledge and skills to do it. His intent was clear: to use the merchant's death as a coercive way to obtain money from my father. The soldier asked for an amount of money that equaled the value of a cow. I do not remember how much my father paid him, but it was enormous. After receiving the money, the soldier returned to his camp. The merchant was buried behind my house because we did not have a cemetery. His merchant peers were notified of his death at least a week later when they returned to my village on the market day.

Some countries have no stable or legitimate legal institutions and systems to serve and protect their citizens. My country is a good example—at least when I was growing up. I have no doubt that such instability and disorder still exist today. Next time you see a police officer, for example, helping you or someone else, let them know how grateful you are for what they do. If you are not grateful, try to visit countries where there is no recourse or legal measures in place when citizens' rights are abused daily. That is why I tell my coworkers in the United States that some Americans are spoiled in thinking police officers mistreat and fail to respect citizens. While there may be plenty of evidence to back such a claim, the point I am making here is that there are worse legal systems in many countries.

Unfortunately, this was not my worst experience with my country's government. Now, I will introduce you to an ethnic conflict that has been ongoing for decades, which forced me to be a political refugee in the United States.

PREVENTED TO MEET THE LIBERATORS

The First Congo War (1996–1997) began as a revolutionary movement to remove a dictator, former President Mobutu. However, the war became more ethnically motivated, and its end exposed the truth about it, which was apparent from late 1998 on. In this section, I will refrain from going into much detail about the political matters at play. My aim here is only to provide context so I can discuss what I experienced in 1996.

In the early 1990s, the Democratic Republic of Congo (when it was still called Zaïre) was going through rough political times. The infamous Transitional Parliament's Vangu Commission was in operation in both Kivu provinces, identifying who was a national and who was not. The Great Lakes of Africa region (also known as the Central African region) was experiencing political turmoil. Rwanda and Burundi had civil wars. Thousands and thousands of refugees from Rwanda and Burundi had fled to Congo. The Vangu Commission was biased, especially toward my ethnic group—the Banyamulenge—and other groups, such as Tutsis and Hutus in North Kivu. It argued that we were not nationals. The commission concluded its identification mission by saying that members of my ethnic group must have been kicked out of the country and calling us foreigners and immigrants even after we'd been in the country for centuries.

The Banyamulenge rejected the commission's conclusions that they were foreigners and decided to defend themselves. Among them were former combatants (Abagiriye), who had fought other ethnic-motivated battles in earlier years. The term Abagiriye was derived from the French word *guerrières*, or warriors. The Abagiriye reactivated themselves. Their original defensive initiative began in the 1960s during the Simba Mulele rebellion, in which all the Banyamulenge families were forced out of their villages. The Abagiriye defended their families and recaptured their villages from the hands of Mai Mai militias.

During the early 1990s, hundreds of Banyamulenge youths joined Rwandan refugees to help them return home from Uganda during their war that began on October 1, 1990. After Rwanda was liberated from former President Juvenal Habyarimana's regime, the Vangu Commission's findings were applied in the eastern Democratic Republic of Congo, forcing all the Banyamulenge out of the country. In a press conference on October 8, 1996, South Kivu Deputy Governor Lwasi Ngabo Lwabanji[9] gave the Banyamulenge seven days to leave the country or be treated as rebels and be militarily attacked. The public announcement from the second citizen of the province shook Banyamulenge families throughout the country. It did not take long for the Banyamulenge to start getting attacked, beheaded, and burned in the streets of the Congo (then Zaïre). Deadly attacks occurred in our villages as well. Mai Mai groups, which were armed civilians from neighboring ethnic groups, carried out the attacks and plundered thousands of herds of cattle belonging to the Banyamulenge.

At that time, dozens of soldiers from the Banyamulenge community, those youths who had gone to help Rwandan refugees return to their country in the early 1990s, had covertly come back to

---

9   "Zaïre: IRIN Update on the Conflict in South Kivu, 10/11/96," United Nations Department of Humanitarian Affairs Integrated Regional Information Network, *University of Pennsylvania – African Studies Center*, October 11, 1996, https://www.africa.upenn.edu/Hornet/irin_101196.html

their villages to rescue their parents. They were scattered throughout the highlands region, hiding and ready to attack each of the national army's camps. There was a date set when the country's military and our neighbors (other ethnic groups) would conduct numerous deadly attacks in Banyamulenge villages.

My village, Bijombo Center, was among the villages with a military camp. We observed that soldiers in it had dug caves around their tents in preparation for the war. During that period, my family had moved from the Bijombo Center to an opposite hill my father had named Ararati (named after the biblical Mount Ararat, on which Noah's ark came to rest after the Great Flood). Only three houses were on this hill: my father's house, my older brother's, and my neighbor's. Because the insecurity had increased in the country, especially in our area, my family moved to another village called Mutara, which was adjacent to Ararati. Bijombo Center, Ararati, and Mutara were three hills that shared one valley.

The war was looming. Each evening, men would gather in one spot to listen to radio broadcasts about what was happening throughout the country and in the entire African Great Lakes region. Some trusted and popular radio stations included the BBC and the Voice of America. We heard horrific news of killings and ambushes in different parts of the country—specifically, in our highlands region. Many Banyamulenge were reportedly beheaded in public, such as in Uvira. Others were still in detention, waiting for execution. Other members of surrounding ethnic groups were also allegedly killed in several areas. Because we lived in a rural area with many bushes and hiding places, people found dead bodies in different corners of the highlands region, not knowing who had killed them. Villagers were terrified and did not know what to do and what would come next.

People stopped grazing cattle far from homes. They brought cows home earlier than usual to avoid ambushes in the late evening hours. Fear was intense. Many people stopped traveling around as they used to because of the insecurity.

My family had moved out of our house on the Ararati hill. But we still had several things left in it, including dry food, such as corn. Because the dry food was in one of the storage areas inside the house (*ku rusenge*), my mother took me to help her get it by climbing the small wooden built-in ladder. The ladder was built near one of the pillars and connected to the storage above the fireplace. While assisting my mother in getting the food from the storage, I heard men's voices from my parents' vacated room. I could not identify them, so I asked my mother who they were. But she distracted me, pretending she did not know them. I immediately realized she did not want to tell me. I had a feeling she knew what was going on in our house. Then, when I got down from the storage, I attempted to open the door to my dad's room to check and find out for myself who was there.

"Stop. Where are you going?" My mother held my hand and made me face the other way. I needed clarification about why she was preventing me from entering the room. I was fourteen and knew she was hiding something from me. That is why I still remember the story.

"Let's go," she said, then made me leave the house, asking me to carry one of the food bags to our new home.

I never questioned why she stopped me from entering their abandoned room. But the secret revealed itself the following morning. The Banyamulenge soldiers who had come back from helping Rwandan refugees returning to their home country, Rwanda, attacked all national military camps in the highlands area to stop the planned deadly attacks on Banyamulenge civilians in their villages. I realized that the voices I had heard in my old house belonged to some of those soldiers. It was a group of about six soldiers led by Section (Squad) Commander Kayoyo, who later became a major general in the current country's military structure, the Democratic Republic of Congo's armed forces. I later understood that they preferred to hide in my old house because it was in an abandoned, remote, small village away from the rest of the most populated villages.

Only a few people in our villages knew about the plan to attack military barracks. The plan was very sensitive, which is why it was kept secret. I still visualize that morning of the attack. The military camp was about a mile east of the Bijombo Center, near the hospital. The area was called Karambi because it was a flat surface. The fight began about five a.m. and lasted the whole day.

At about seven a.m., we saw about four male individuals in tan trench coats. They were walking with their heads down, flanking the military camp area with AK-47s. Adults advised they were the Banyamulenge soldiers fighting the national army. Bullets started coming our way from the military camp. The entire village ran into the bush on the other side of the hill. Only some adults could go back into the village to bring families food.

These early attacks consisted of an extended plan shared by many Congolese to topple President Mobutu's regime. Laurent-Désiré Kabila became the movement's leader. The war expanded, and in less than a year, Mobutu's government was no longer. The rebellion deposed President Mobutu on May 17, 1997, after the capital city of Kinshasa was captured. This ended the First Congo War.

Ethnic-driven conflict in the Democratic Republic of Congo remains a serious issue today. It has devasted the country and its inhabitants. Millions have died as a result. Thousands and thousands of people from all ethnic groups have been living in multiple countries as political refugees for decades. Many efforts, including those initiated by the United Nations, have provided no solutions. Any discrimination, including ethnic-motived discrimination, is a virus that ruins communities. Have you experienced any discrimination? Specifically, racial or ethnic? If so, what was your reaction?

I began this chapter with a story of how my thirteen-year-old and six-year-old American-born daughters were surprised when I told them about my childhood life in Bijombo, how I grew up without contemporary technologies, and how my village had no roads, bicycles, vehicles, or electricity. Fifna was born in California, and Faith was born in Texas. They knew I was not born in the United States. I had told them I was from the Congo. However, they had no idea what my early life experience looked like. They also never experienced being an immigrant.

If you are reading this book as an immigrant like me, you might have grown up in a similar village setting. Your village's composition and structure might or might not have been identical to mine. I wanted to share my childhood story and show where and how I began. If you are not an immigrant and were born and grew up in a developed city or non-village setting, I hope my humble beginning provides an inspirational spirit to get you going and defeat procrastination and other setbacks in life, including excuses.

The first chapter ends with my experience with the First Congo War in 1996, how the dictator's military camps were attacked in our villages to prevent a planned genocide, and how the dictator was removed from power. Chapter 2 will give you a glance at the second part of my life outside my village. It will describe my journey from Bijombo to Uvira, a city on the shores of Lake Tanganyika in the eastern Democratic Republic of Congo, where I spent at least eight years. It will introduce you to how, as a fourteen-year-old boy, I managed to cross a guerrilla movement's roadblock that intended to force teenagers and young adults into its revolutionary warfare.

CHAPTER 2

MY UNFULFILLED DREAMS AND HOPES

*We stand today on the edge of a new frontier—the frontier of the
1960s—a frontier of unknown opportunities and perils—
a frontier of unfulfilled hopes and threats.*
– John F. Kennedy

It's unfulfilled dreams that keep you alive.
– Robert H. Schuller

A VILLAGE BOY ENTERING A CITY FOR THE FIRST TIME

T he First Congo War caused my family to move from my home
village, Bijombo, to the city of Uvira, a coastal town on the
west edge of Lake Tanganyika. I did not know of other things that
might have prompted my parents to make such an unexpected decision. Moving from a village to a city was a significant change. Most
things in Uvira were new to me, including the beautiful view of
Lake Tanganyika, the asphalt of the city's one and only paved street,
and the unique smell of the town, which I had never experienced

before. I quickly realized that the scent was coming from restaurants, businesses, and other things, including air pollution that contained numerous biochemical substances, such as smoke from gas and diesel engines. Even the water of Lake Tanganyika smelled different from my home village's waters. The city was polluted because it was in the valley between elevated mountains and a lake.

Figure 2.1: A giant mountain leading to my home village
One of the enormous mountains (Kirungwa) leads to my village from Uvira. Even today, these mountains have no roads. Therefore, people walk up and down for hours to travel between villages in the highlands region and the city of Uvira.
Ngabo

In October 1996, I was fourteen years old. Descending the steep mountain of Kataka, one of the high mountains west of Uvira, to reach the town was an enormous challenge for a fourteen-year-old who had not experienced it before. I had not been to Uvira before, and I was both excited and intimidated. At the same time, it was during the First Congo War. The situation was intense. The country was on fire, with the sounds of heavy guns in different corners. A few days earlier, Uvira had fallen into the hands of a new guerrilla movement, the Alliance of Democratic Forces for the Liberation of Congo-Zaïre (known for its French acronym of AFDL), which was fighting to overthrow Zaïre's long-lasting President Joseph Mobutu.

Our journey from Bijombo to Uvira lasted about two days on foot, climbing mountains with no roads and descending others. There was a group of us traveling together. The trip was tiring for a fourteen-year-old. My legs were sore, and my feet suffered blisters, making wearing my rough and uncomfortable rubber shoes difficult and painful.

We came to a military roadblock a little over a mile above the town. These were AFDL soldiers who had captured the city. They had different mentalities from Zaïre's soldiers and were just different from their counterparts. Even their firearms and uniforms looked different. Also, the AFDL soldiers spoke Swahili and other local dialects, whereas the former regime's soldiers spoke Lingala in a threatening manner. Swahili was commonly used by the local population, and Lingala was primarily used by Zaïre's soldiers, so it was interpreted as a soldiers' language. Therefore, because Zaïre's soldiers had developed a culture of threatening, mistreating, harassing, beating, and looting citizens, the Lingala language was perceived as threatening. However, the AFDL soldiers were also not easy on the population. They abused civilians as well.

As expected, they stopped us. Their job was to stop and question anyone coming through their roadblock. At this time, because of the new war that had just started, the revolutionary movement was interested in youth joining the rebellion. Young men who did not want to join the movement's military branch hid from soldiers. On this trip to Uvira, I was with teenagers my age who appeared to be adults because they were taller than me. One of them was my childhood friend, Aimable. Others were a little older than us but were still minors, although their sizes made them look like adults.

Before we approached the roadblock, we had learned that soldiers were likely to keep teenagers they thought would be fit for the military and force them to join the new movement (*urufato*). Those teenagers with us who appeared to be young adults, including Aimable, wore a type of cloth (*kitenge* in Swahili) worn by girls and women so they could pretend to be girls. I didn't pretend because of how small I was. I kept wearing my shorts. In our culture, only children and teenagers were supposed to wear shorts. We managed to pass the roadblock without difficulties and arrived in Uvira.

Figure 2.2: Another huge mountain leading to my home village
This is the Kataka mountain, another way to my home village. The picture was taken from Uvira, the first town my family moved to in 1996 during the First Congo War.
Ngabo

It was my first time seeing many things in a city setting. After growing up in a poor village without running water, roads, vehicles, motorcycles, bicycles, electricity, or other essential technologies, the first thing I noticed was the city's asphalt road. When I looked at it from a distance on a sunny day, it appeared to have glass or some liquid in the middle. But, after I reached the location, the glass or water I'd seen from far away disappeared.

Uvira's culture was different from Bijombo's in the way people talked, the language they spoke, the clothes they wore, what they ate, and much more. To some degree, the difference was due to the majority of villagers in Bijombo being Banyamulenge, meaning I was used to surrounding myself with my ethnic group members. In Uvira, however, there were multiple tribes. The Banyamulenge were among the minorities. Even the Banyamulenge who lived in Uvira appeared different from those in Bijombo.

Generally speaking, Uvira's environment differed from that of Bijombo. For example, during the day, there was noise from welding shops and smells from different sources, including restaurants. Even the smell of polluted air in Uvira convinced me I was in a better place and life. I quickly forgot the unpolluted, fresh air in my home village. Regardless, I needed to leave my undeveloped village to improve my education and life.

I hope you can now understand that I experienced life challenges worth sharing. If you can relate to my story, remember to be thankful for what you have or where you came from. If you never experienced what I experienced, then be grateful you did not.

In the following section, I will discuss my meeting with my brother, who had left my village in response to a call for military service in the revolutionary movement.

LOSING MY BROTHER TO FREEDOM FIGHTING

My brother answered a call for military service in the AFDL in 1996, when we still lived in Bijombo. The family had no news of his whereabouts. Many families in our villages longed to reunite with their sons who had gone to different places to fight for their freedom. The AFDL was a powerful movement that deprived thousands of young men of their normal lives, including education and marriage. Even married young men left their brides and children to fight for their families' liberation.

My brother Rutaramirwa, whom I was born after, was an extremely reticent person. He did not easily reveal his thoughts to others. It was hard to know when he was happy or sad. He kept his things to himself. He was simply different in our family. Like other young people, he joined the revolutionary movement to fight the Mobutu regime in 1996. When we moved from our village to Uvira in the same year, we learned his deployment was in the same city. We quickly knew where he was positioned.

One morning, after the war was finished in Uvira but was still going in other cities throughout the country, my parents and I met him at a military roadblock. He was on his shift. He asked a fellow soldier to take his spot as he spoke with us. He walked us off the roadblock and promised to come to our house in Uvira for an extended visit the following day.

Uvira was still suffering from the aftermath of the war. Everything was chaotic, including the military movements and unfamiliar faces of soldiers in the city. The fight was in the Baraka area, south of Uvira. Soldiers had severe restrictions, especially when it came to moving freely in the town without their superiors' permission (*kibali* in Swahili). Those who violated the restriction were immediately arrested and sent to the battlefront (*kuzowa*, a military term at that time). We were later told that's what happened to my brother when he tried to come to our house without permission from his immediate commander.

He tried to fulfill his promise by coming to see us that morning. His reasoning for not asking permission, whether or not that was the case, remains unknown. Even the explanation for why he did not make it home remains unverified because we never had the chance to talk to him after that day at the roadblock. We hardly heard about him afterward. News about his possible death came in 1998, during the Second Congo War. The news about him being killed in an ambush was never verified either. As of today, the family still suspects he may be alive because of his reserved character.

I have never heard from him since that day he promised to visit. It is a shocking, lifetime pain to lose a sibling without being able to bury him. He was like others—attempting to fulfill his moral obligation to be part of a military movement to topple a dictator for the sake of his people's freedom.

Have you lost a sibling or a significant other in a similar mysterious situation? If you have, I feel you. If you have not, be thankful that you have not gone through such an experience.

STRUGGLING TO PAY A MONTHLY SCHOOL FEE OF TWO DOLLARS

Despite the heartbreaking experience of my brother's disappearance, I had a task waiting for me: to learn a city's way of life.

Life in Uvira was different from life in a village. The city setting was complicated and intimidating. I felt lost amid people who spoke

Swahili, a language I thought I knew, but in a manner different from what I was used to. I quickly found myself faking to fit into the new community. Sometimes, faking failed to work. But I persisted, hoping to master the new culture and feel at home.

It did not take long to realize that I needed to learn many things about this new setting. The primary language for ordinary, public communication was Swahili. I had spoken a little Swahili in Bijombo only when I met and spoke with someone who did not speak my mother tongue, Kinyamulenge. People who visited or stayed in Bijombo for a short period either had to learn my language to communicate or use Swahili to speak with villagers who spoke it. In Uvira, Swahili was the main language. Although I did not struggle with it, using the language daily felt weird.

The first house we lived in had a fence. I acquired a bicycle from someone I do not remember. The next step was to learn how to ride it. A friend gave me instructions on how to efficiently operate it. I practiced on my own inside our house's fenced area. There was enough room to make circles, so I made countless rounds. Once I felt comfortable, I rode it on the public street.

Another exciting activity was swimming in the lake. I had basic swimming skills from Bijombo, where I practiced swimming in small rivers, especially whenever it rained and filled the rivers. I used the basic swimming skills from Bijombo in Lake Tanganyika and learned more about swimming in this lake. We swam in its deep waters. One day, a motorboat almost struck us while we were swimming. We would have been smashed if some of us had not stayed on the shore to alert the speedboat to our presence.

I left Bijombo when I was in eighth grade. Schools in Uvira intimidated me, and I assumed that schools in villages did not provide adequate education like those in cities. That is why I decided to go back to sixth grade in Uvira. No school made me do it. No one influenced me either. It was my own decision. I later realized it was not a good decision and regretted that I made it. My suspicions about the school village were not correct.

I registered at Action Kusaidia in sixth grade. My teacher was called Maître Kitenge. We took the final exam in sixth grade, called *concours,* or competition, and I obtained the certificate (primary school diploma). The Action Kusaidia's school system was a tough one, and it was considered one of the few top primary schools in Uvira with better education.

Figure 2.3: My Sixth grade at Action Kusaidia Institute
This was my sixth-grade class at Action Kusaidia Institute in the city of Uvira, the Democratic Republic of Congo. The picture was taken during the 1996–1997 school year.
Unknown

Compared to other schools in town, my school had many strict rules. Regarding the uniform, students were required to wear a white shirt and blue pants, which was the primary uniform for most schools in Congo. At Action Kusaidia, it was a must for students to tuck in their shirts. A tie was also part of the uniform requirements. Students who were late for school were punished severely. Those who failed to stop wherever they were while the national anthem was sung were punished. We referred to our principal as a coordinator. He was very strict and not friendly toward students. The school had a director of discipline (DD). However, the coordinator took charge of punishing students. I purposely say "punishing" because the way he disciplined students was unspeakable. He kept the metal main piece of an umbrella in his office, and his style was to strike the back of students' hands. He made students enter his office and shut the door behind him. Then he asked each student one at a time to flip their hands, showing the back side and extending the hand to him. Students held out one hand at a time, switching both hands to balance the inflicted pain. In doing so, one hand would take a break while the other was being struck. He hit the back of the hand with full force several times. He did not care about fracturing the bones. The punishment occurred while students were on their knees, making it difficult for them to get away from him.

I spent sixth and seventh grades at Action Kusaidia before moving to Kimanga Institute for the eighth through twelfth grades. Kimanga Institute was different from Action Kusaidia. Its school system had a lesser reputation than Action Kusaidia's. The uniform was a white shirt and blue pants. A tie was not required. Tucked-in shirts were not enforced either. Like other schools, the high school demanded that students bring different things to benefit the school and teachers as a form of discipline. Requiring students to bring items from home as a type of a disciplinary measure was one thing that related one school to the other. Simply put, Kimanga Institute was laid-back regarding strict rules and teaching.

I attended Kimanga Institute because I wanted to study biology and chemistry. However, the school had no laboratories for students to practice and do science experiments. The school needed more financial resources and could not afford a laboratory and science equipment. Students studied only those subjects that required laboratory in theory, reading what was supposed to happen in practice.

Figure 2.4: Action Kusaidia Institute 28 years later
Action Kusaidia Institute today. The picture was taken in March 2024.
Ngabo

I struggled to finish high school for several reasons. First, my parents had difficulty paying my monthly school fees because they had no jobs. My father worked part-time at the border at one time. At other times, I do not know how he supported our family. The monthly school fee at Kimanga Institute was two dollars. It was challenging to get the money every month to pay my school tuition and my sister's. My older sister who lived in Rwanda assisted paying for my tuition.

Another challenge was a problem with my vision. I became sick toward the end of the school year in twelfth grade. I had difficulty seeing the writing on the blackboard, which was the sole tool used to allow students to take notes. We did not have individual books to learn from. Teachers even used former students' notebooks from previous years to teach current students. If the old notebooks had missing materials or contained errors, students learning from them had no way to correct the errors because the student who took the notes was nowhere to be found.

To address my vision issue, I moved to the front seat in the classroom. I still had problems clearly seeing the blackboard from the front seat, though the distance was about eight feet. I stood up, moved to the blackboard, read the writing, and returned to the desk to copy what I had read in my notebook. It was tiring and took me an enormous amount of time to stay on track with other students. Most of the time, I borrowed notebooks from fellow students after class to finish taking notes. The only option I had was to quit school to seek treatment.

Because Uvira had no eye doctors, I went to Burundi and Rwanda, two neighboring countries to the east, to seek vision treatment so I could return to school. Unfortunately, I did not receive adequate treatment because of the lack of money. I received only a bottle of eye drops. I do not remember the name of the medication. After obtaining it, I returned to Uvira and used it for a few weeks, but it did not bring my vision back.

Leaving school at this stage in my education was challenging, as it conflicted with the state exam that was required to graduate from twelfth grade. The exam was taken once a year. Students who failed did not pass the grade and had to retake the test if they wanted a diploma. They were only required to retake the exam once a year until they passed. Otherwise, they missed the chance to continue their education in college. The test application process involved filling out physical forms and sending them to Kinshasa, the capital city, thousands of miles away. The next step was taking the state test. The exam was a tough one. Students had to prepare for it by isolating themselves in a private location, away from home, to study for months before the testing day.

When I left my school and Uvira for eye treatment, I still needed to complete the graduation application. I stopped going to school for at least three months. When I came back from Burundi and Rwanda, I realized I had missed the deadline to apply for graduation. My classmates had already gone to a private location to study for the national exam. I spoke with my principal about my situation, and he gave me the form to fill out. It was impossible to send a digital copy of the document from Uvira to Kinshasa. There was no such thing as an Internet-based platform to send or upload documents digitally. The form had to be taken by vehicle from Uvira to Bukavu (the provincial capital) and then go to Kinshasa via airplane. My form was sent after the deadline, and I did not have hope that it would reach the Ministry of Education office before the exam day. But I joined my classmates to prepare for the exam anyway, even though they had been studying for months. I was behind in everything.

My chances of doing well on the national test were slim. First, I was preparing for the exam without knowing if my application had reached its destination. Communication in the Congo was difficult. It was impossible to give the Ministry of Education a phone call to check the status of my application. I had to wait for the final list of students eligible to take the exam to be published through my school.

As the test day approached, I learned from my principal that my name had appeared on the final list. I took it as a miracle. I took the exam without hoping to pass because I had missed many days of schooling due to the problem with my eyes.

I considered it God's miracle that I passed the national exam and obtained my high school diploma in biochemistry in 2003. I was among the four students who passed the test at Kimanga Institute. The others were Mubangu Mulombe, Mudagiri Janvier, and Ndayikunda Nkurunziza. Thirty students applied for the national exam in twelfth grade at my high school. Twenty-nine took the examination, and one failed to attend on the exam day. Except for Mudagiri, who obtained his diploma at 51 percent, the rest of us obtained our diplomas at 50 percent (equivalent to 2.0 American grade point average), the minimum percentage needed to pass the high school national exam in the Congo.

Getting a high school diploma in the Congo was a big deal. It was not something to take for granted. People who knew my struggle did not believe what God had done for me. I felt like I did not deserve the high school diploma that year because of the health circumstances described above. That is why I took it as a miracle.

Now you understand how difficult my life was in the Congo. Imagine being a parent and struggling to earn two dollars a month for your children's school fees. Although I had difficulty with my vision during the national exam preparation, which forced me to fall behind in the preparation process, I was surprised to obtain the high school diploma. Most people struggled with that exam, regardless of the enormous effort and time they invested in getting ready. I was the lucky one.

Remember my story the next time you struggle with something. Do not be discouraged. Also, do not complain about not having the extra things you do not even need. I hope it will help you be grateful for what you already have.

Now, let us explore a social and political challenge: ethnic discrimination.

EXPOSED TO ETHNIC DISCRIMINATION IN MY COUNTRY

In Uvira, discrimination occurred in many forms. They called us Rwandans, referring to the same reason discussed above. But the residents of Uvira from other ethnic communities had sophisticated ways to marginalize us. For instance, they insulted all members of my community, arguing that we all walked with open mouths, which was far from the truth. "*Funga kinywa*," or "Close your mouth," they said to the Banyamulenge people whenever they ran into them. They emphasized this insult by saying that members of the Banyamulenge community had come to the city (Uvira) from villages (Bijombo and elsewhere in the mountains above Uvira) and always left their mouths open, suggesting that having an open mouth was due to having come from undeveloped villages. The insult damaged the self-esteem of the

Banyamulenge people. A person with a closed mouth would still feel embarrassed even if the insult had nothing to do with them.

Another form of discrimination against members of the Banyamulenge ethnic group was based on their accent. Members of other communities who enjoyed discriminating us used the letter *R* to refer to the members of the Banyamulenge community, claiming that the Banyamulenge did not know how to differentiate *R* from *L*, as in *Congolais*, or *Congolese*. They would emphasize the last syllable, *-lais*, and make it *-rais* to make it sound horrible ("Congorais" instead of Congolais; unfortunately, this discriminatory practice still exists today). They sang this repeatedly to indicate that all Banyamulenge pronounced in that manner. As a result of the insults, some members of the Banyamulenge community in Uvira began staying away from their members who were freshly arrived from villages. In other words, they fell into traps and began to deny their own. They discriminated against themselves to disassociate from their ethnic community to avoid facing discrimination from the general population. Most of the time, this strategy failed to work because all members of the Banyamulenge were still considered the same regardless.

I have learned that discrimination is contagious, like a virus. Once they have been successfully discriminated against, a person tends to discriminate against others, starting with those subject to the same discrimination. If you hate injustice, become an activist to fight discrimination.

Next, I will explain the negative impact of such discrimination in the Congo.

POLITICAL INSTABILITY THROUGHOUT THE YEARS

Discrimination against the Banyamulenge and other similar ethnic minority groups in the country was the cause of continuous instability over many years. When a section of citizens chooses to hate those they believe to be different, the result is obvious: they kill them and plunder their wealth. However, the citizens who are discriminated against find several means of defending themselves. That is what has been happening in the Congo for many decades, specifically concerning the Banyamulenge.

As a reminder, my family moved to Uvira in 1996 after Uvira and other major cities in the Eastern Congo had fallen into the arms of the AFDL during the First Congo War. The first war was called revolutionary because it aimed to topple long-lasting President Mobutu, and it did in May 1997. However, it did not take long for the Second Congo War to erupt in August 1998.

In the First Congo War, the leader on the side of the revolutionists was Laurent-Désiré Kabila. The First Congo War was also referred to as the "Banyamulenge Rebellion" because one of the AFDL's motives was said to be liberating the Banyamulenge people from enduring discrimination and persecution in Zaïre. It should be highlighted that Laurent-Désiré Kabila, who was now claiming to rescue the Banyamulenge, was one of the influential Mai Mai leaders in the 1960s who attacked the Banyamulenge in their home villages. The Second Congo War began because those who had fought the First Congo War disagreed on things the general population never understood. The war quickly shifted and became between the Tutsi people in the Eastern Congo and the rest of the Congolese population. But the war was more political than it appeared, and other members from various ethnic groups joined the new rebellion.

During the Second Congo War, in 1998, my family members and others fled Uvira. I returned to my home village, Bijombo. After the war, the family was reunited in Uvira. Four years later, in 2002, a coalition of several Congolese armed groups invaded and captured Uvira for a few days from the south. The city had been in the hands of the Congolese Rally for Democracy (known by its French acronym of RCD). It was the time to flee again.

This time, my parents and sister fled to Burundi to what became, in 2004, the Gatumba refugee camp. (I will discuss the Gatumba refugee camp in more detail later.) Banyamulenge families in Uvira referred to the first time they fled to Gatumba in 2002 as Gatumba 1, and the second time in 2004 as Gatumba 2. During Gatumba 1, the refugees stayed for only a few days and then returned to their homes. During Gatumba 2, various armed groups in the region attacked them inside the camp, killing and injuring hundreds.

During the war of 2002, I stayed in Uvira with other Banyamulenge members who stayed behind. I was the only one in my family who did not flee. Some families and individuals failed to flee on time. Therefore, it was too late for them to leave the city and go toward Burundi. The only way to escape was to climb the mountains west of Uvira and head toward our home villages in the highlands region.

One morning, gunshots increased throughout the town. The gunfight was active on both sides. A group of us left a home we were staying in near Action Kusaidia (my school) and ran toward the school. As we were running and ducking in the street between the house and school, gunshots increased even more, as if they were fighting within feet of us on the other side of the fence. We ducked more and ran right back to the house. It was chaos, and people were confused. Nobody in the group seemed to know where we were going when we decided to leave the home. So, we moved from house to house, trying to hide from the rebels.

A day or two later, unknown people shot my neighbor, Mzee Muyuku, in his house. At this time, the city was already under the rebels' control. Guns were everywhere, and civilians who carried them were uncontrolled. A few of us transported the wounded, elderly Muyuku to the city's general hospital. He was shot in the stomach, and we wrapped a loincloth around his abdomen to stop the bleeding. We put him on a bike and pushed him to the hospital, which took about twenty minutes.

The medical facility was not close to where Mzee Muyuku lived. He lived in the Kimanga neighborhood, right above the main roadway to the Zone (a neighborhood by the shores of the lake). We pushed him on the bicycle past the Monument (a neighborhood north of Kimanga) to the general hospital. We did not have a car to transport him. Luckily, the heavy gunshots had stopped. We could still hear one here and there throughout the town. The regular traffic had not been established yet. Unfortunately, because we had no adequate training or equipment to treat a wound, especially a gunshot wound, Mzee Muyuku passed away before we reached the hospital. We continued pushing him to the hospital so doctors could pronounce him dead. It was apparent he died on the bicycle. He stopped breathing and talking to us. That is when we knew he was no longer with us.

I have learned that discrimination against an ethnic group leads to chaotic and deadly incidents among different groups. Any discrimination leads to more problems rather than solutions. Be part of the solution rather than the problem.

Now I will discuss how I moved from Uvira to Bukavu to attend college, though I could not finish it due to political instability.

ATTENDING A MEDICAL TRAINING COLLEGE WITH NO CHANCE TO FINISH IT

After I graduated from Kimanga Institute, it was time to find a college institution in the region. Uvira's few colleges were small, had bad reputations, and did not teach what I wanted to study. I had a high school diploma in biochemistry, even though my high school did not have laboratories for science experiments and hands-on practice, and I still had the spirit of studying science in college. Because I wanted to be in the medical field, my only option was to go to bigger cities in my own country or neighboring countries.

I realized it would be more expensive to go outside the country. Going to the country's capital city, Kinshasa, would also be more expensive. Bukavu was the only feasible option because a family member offered to pay for my college fees. So, I found a medical college in Bukavu, the provincial capital of South Kivu, around seventy-eight miles north of the city of Uvira, called ISTM (Institut Supérieur des Techniques Médicales, or High Institute of Medical Techniques). I also found a place to stay with some family members in Bukavu while attending ISTM. I received admission into the laboratory techniques major and wanted to be a *laborantin*, or lab technician.

I started attending ISTM sometime in October 2003. Other students had already begun in September of that year. I was late. Congolese colleges and universities allowed public bullying of new students. I missed the big day—the freshman hazing day—when all new students were collectively and mercilessly hazed. However, the students did not let me go free. In a classroom of about two hundred students, where it was a daily challenge to find a seat, the students knew an invader, a newcomer, was in the house. To them, I was a new student who had not been bullied yet and needed particular attention.

The classroom was packed, so taking notes from the blackboard was competitive. The students struggled to see the writing on the blackboard from where they sat or stood (not everyone had a place to sit). Most of the time, I stood in the back. I did not have enough influence to gain a seat, mainly because I was still a candidate for hazing. My eye condition had grown worse, and I still needed a vision treatment. I went home almost every day without finishing taking notes. I had to borrow other students' notes to catch up.

One morning, when the professor exited the classroom, it was my turn to face individual hazing. The students circled me inside the classroom. They pushed me around to each other while yelling at me and calling me different names. They intimidated me by accusing me of being a Rwandan and insulted me by calling me a Rwandais, or Rwandan. One of them had a Rwandan franc bill. They asked me if I could exchange it for Congolese francs. They emphasized I could because the Rwandan francs were my home currency—they were not. I said I could not exchange the money. They screamed some more and threatened me with severe bodily injury.

Then they picked one of the female students and got her closer to me. She extended her face toward me, giving me her cheek. Other students began yelling and asking me to kiss her on the cheek. I refused. They screamed some more in a threatening manner. They pushed me around and toward the female student, forcing me to kiss her cheek. I still hesitated and resisted. I knew it was a trap. They laid their hands on me and bumped me into the girl. I felt confused and terrorized. This time, I decided to kiss her cheek to avoid potential bodily harm. When they realized I was about to kiss her, she distanced herself from me. The crowd pointed fingers at me and repeatedly yelled in Swahili, "*Utazala umu weye*," or "You will have babies in here." I had never felt embarrassed before the way I did that morning. I became ashamed of myself and felt diminished to the point of avoiding eye contact with other students.

God does wonders. A male student in the crowd must have been unable to stand the harassment I was facing and seen I was about to get more. He jumped in front of the other students and stretched his arms between them and me. He ordered them to stop bullying me. They attempted to ignore his command at first, but miraculously, they obeyed him and abandoned their bullying. He appeared to have influenced them even though he was small. I could have thanked that student and rewarded him, but I did not know him and was scared to approach him after the fact. However, I owed him respect and love for the remainder of the days I attended ISTM.

Figure 2.5: ISTM in Bukavu
The picture was taken in March 2024.
Olivier

The freshman hazing was one thing, but discrimination against members of the Banyamulenge ethnic community at the college continued even after the hazing period, which was the first few weeks of the first year. Discrimination against my community affected how I was bullied. Though hazing was a permissible practice for first-year students in colleges and universities in the Congo, my treatment was unique because I was regarded as a foreigner in my country. I realized I was bullied mainly by students who resented my ethnic group. I encourage you to avoid associating with practices that belittle others because they are thought to be different.

Meanwhile, insecurity-related tension grew progressively day after day, month after month, between regional military commanders General Prosper Nabyolwa (and later General Mbuza Mabe) and their deputy, Colonel Jules Mutebutsi. Colonel Mutebutsi was a member of the Banyamulenge community, while others were not. As tensions were growing, my friends and I were renting a small single-room house in the college neighborhood of Karhale. We stayed at school during weekdays and visited our families in town on weekends. Those visits included church services on Sundays. A gunfight erupted later between the commanders mentioned above, forcing all schools in Bukavu to close.

In the following section, I will expand on the political and military turmoil between these national army commanders, which might have stemmed from numerous reasons, including ethnic conflict and differences.

A RAIN OF BULLETS AND BOMBS BEGAN FALLING

Ethnic violence and conflict in the Congo became intense year after year. Ethnic-motivated political deadly events became a practice. It had become a norm for military commanders to side with their ethnic groups as a way to protect their communities' interests—specifically, political and security ones. Because of chronic discrimination against the Banyamulenge, soldiers from this ethnic community remained alert and refused to put their guard down. Defensively, soldiers from the Banyamulenge ethnic group reacted when they felt their community was targeted, threatened as a whole, and labeled as foreigners, Rwandans, refugees, immigrants, and other unpleasant names, which singled them out for persecution in their deployments.

Colonel Jules Mutebutsi had been deployed to Bukavu as the regional military deputy commander of General Prosper Nabyolwa, and then General Mbuza Mabe, who relieved General Nabyolwa in the middle of the conflict. Mutebutsi was in Uvira as a brigadier commander of the 9th Brigade. It was reported that the conflict between the two top commanders of South Kivu, General Nabyolwa and Colonel Mutebutsi, stemmed from the fact that RCD-Goma (Rally for Congolese Democracy-Goma) did not want a search for their hidden arsenal in Bukavu. Another given reason was that a military officer accused of killing former President Laurent-Désiré Kabila was hiding in Bukavu. It was said that the RCD-Goma was not ready to deliver him to the Kinshasa regime for prosecution. Colonel Jules Mutebutsi was a former officer of the RCD-Goma. Regardless of what caused the conflict, nobody could resolve the growing political issue that later took innocent lives.

A few months before this conflict began between the military leaders in Bukavu, discrimination against members of the Banyamulenge community and the Tutsi people in general intensified throughout the Eastern Congo. This affected the daily lives of Banyamulenge students at ISTM and surrounding institutions. I lived in the ISTM's neighborhood of Karhale to stay close to school. The college was located on a giant mountain above the city. The walk from ISTM to downtown Bukavu was significant. Whenever the tension was high in Bukavu, we, the Banyamulenge students, would descend the hill to our families in the city for safety. Whenever the tension was low, we would return to stay near the school.

When I ceased living in Karhale because of the insecurity, I found a place in my sister-in-law's household in the Camp Sayo neighborhood. Sandra (I will use this common name to protect her identity) understood my struggle and warmly welcomed me into her home. She had other family members staying in her house with her children. Whenever it was calm in the city, I would walk from Camp Sayo to ISTM every day to attend classes. It was a long walk, but I still hoped my dream of becoming a lab technician would someday come true.

Unfortunately, it never did. This back-and-forth routine did not last long. It was interrupted for good by the real battle between the commanders in May 2004.

Heavy gunshots started throughout the city on the evening of Wednesday, May 26, 2004, while I was visiting my cousin's family at Nyawera. I had to go back home to my sister-in-law's house. I remembered that Sandra was still out and the children were alone at home. Other adults in the house had gone, some to a choir rehearsal. I felt the urgency to return home as soon as I could. I said goodbye to my cousin's family. Some advised me to stay because the tension was so high and the noise of guns covered the city. The pressure was high because a few people were outside and rushed into their homes for safety. But the urgency to go back to Sandra's house grew even more.

I exited my cousin's house and walked down the half-dark road toward Place Mulamba. Here, at Place Mulamba, resided Colonel Simba Hussein, one of the influential army commanders in town fighting against Colonel Jules Mutebutsi. I heard multiple gunshots coming from Colonel Simba's residence as I was approaching it. I met with Madeberi, a soldier from the Banyamulenge ethnic community who was in plain clothes and coming from Place Mulamba. We did not talk because we did not personally know each other. We passed each other on a narrow street that evening. Strikingly, I later learned that he was shot dead on the same roadway where we met. After passing him, I made a right turn through houses because I wanted to avoid going straight toward Colonel Simba's residence, where gunshots were being fired. The small street between houses took me to the main roadway at the Philadelphia Church. Then I descended into the Camp Sayo valley at Sandra's house.

Fortunately, I found Sandra at the house. She advised she had just arrived. The children had been alone at home. That day was like the day of the biblical Noah's Ark. We locked the front and back metal doors with deadbolts and hoped to open the doors soon after the battle was over. But unfortunately, the other adults in the house never made it home that evening. They got stuck where they were when the conflict started and had to stay in place until it was over.

Then, a rain of bullets and bombs began falling outside. General Mbuza Mabe's soldiers in the Camp Sayo military base on top of the hill above our house were sending their rounds and bombs across the valley to Nguba Market and College Alfajiri, where Colonel Mutebutsi's troops were. The returning fire from Colonel Mutebutsi's troops passed above our house and went into the Camp Sayo base. Some misfired bombs fell in the valley near our home.

After ethnic discrimination penetrates citizens' hearts, it becomes easier to see others as enemies. National cohesion seemed impossible. A country's political matters should not involve ethnic groups. Politicians should refrain from using different ethnic communities to advance their agendas because, after winning or losing their political races, the hatred sowed in citizens continues. Instead of being part of the conflict, you can choose to be an agent to help bring unity to your community or country.

During the 2004 gunfight, I was trapped in the house for two days and two nights. I elaborate on this in the following section.

MAKING EYE CONTACT WITH DEATH BUT GETTING AWAY FROM IT

The 2004 conflict in Bukavu affected and targeted members of the Banyamulenge community, killing dozens of them. Some families found themselves trapped in houses, waiting to be attacked or killed, or hoping to escape. It was a hostage situation. Many families found it difficult to run away from bullets and bombs to save their lives. As a terrible result, several could not escape and were killed in their homes.

My sister-in-law Sandra, her children, and I spent two nights (Wednesday, May 26, and Thursday, May 27) in a locked house, stuck between two heavily armed forces in an active gunfight. Members of the Banyamulenge community were targeted by General Nabyolwa's and General Mbuza Mabe's troops, as well as some civilians from other ethnic communities who had determined to harm them. At this point, dozens had already been slaughtered in different neighborhoods, including Labotte. There were some Banyamulenge families on the Camp Sayo hill above our house, below the military base. I later learned they were invaded, and only Banyamulenge residents were executed. Our house was built on the east creek's edge below the Camp Sayo hill. A small roadway on the house's east side led to other city neighborhoods north and south of our residence.

The fight continued all night on Wednesday. Many residences lost power that night. We did not have electricity in the house, and our phones died. We had no way to communicate with the outside world. We could not come out. We were uncertain of what was happening. The only sounds we could hear were those of guns from both sides. We could not sleep. Sandra led us in prayer, asking God for protection. For some reason, I was not that scared. I felt confident I would not die—not because of the prayer, but because I believed God had plans for my life.

The battle continued on Thursday morning. A few people in the city managed to move around. Sandra had a coworker friend who lived in another neighborhood. The coworker belonged to the Bembe ethnic community. He became worried about our well-being. He sent a messenger to Sandra to find out if we were still alive. His message was twofold. He also wanted to warn us of a potential imminent attack that was being planned for our house on Thursday night. The coworker was specific that the attack's planners had revealed their evil plan, arguing that they knew our house was the only residence still occupied by the Banyamulenge in the entire neighborhood. Their mission was to ensure no Banyamulenge people still lived in the city.

We still had no communication with other Banyamulenge families to know what was happening elsewhere. Our phones were still dead. We still had no electricity to recharge them. We could not move from our house to other city areas to link with our people. Other Banyamulenge members could not come to our rescue. It seemed like we were under house arrest. We had received severe and legitimate warnings from a friend who cared about our safety, but we could not move to avoid the attack. The only option was to stay in the locked house, waiting for our fate. Along with the dead phones, food was diminishing, though we had no time to think about being hungry.

Thursday night, the gunfight intensified. It looked like the fighters on both sides preferred to fight at night. Around seven or eight p.m., as Sandra's coworker had warned, an unknown band of individuals surrounded our house. They dragged machetes on the ground and struck them on our metal doors, calling us out.

"We know you are inside," they said. "Your people have been killed, and others have fled to Rwanda. No Banyamulenge are left in Bukavu. We know you have guns in there. Come out now."

They continued striking their machetes on the front and back doors. They broke the rear window of the kids' bedroom. The children were in the room when this happened. Fortunately, the attackers did not enter through the broken window. It appeared they could not break down the metal doors. We were lucky they did not have or throw grenades into the kids' room.

I was in the hallway, watching both doors for possible entry. I was ready to defend myself and the family, even if I had to die in the process. I had no options other than self-defense.

Then, for some reason, the attackers stopped damaging the house and left. However, they came back hours later, and the same thing happened. They kept screaming in Swahili, "*Mutoke inje mwe Banyarwanda. Tunajua kama muko na bunduki. Leo njo leo. Tutawavusha leo kwenu Rwanda.*" The statement translates to "Come out, you Rwandans. We know you have guns. Today is the day. We will make you go to your home, Rwanda."

We never said a word back to them.

Luckily, on Friday morning, May 28, we remained alive. Some people managed to move around in neighborhoods. We opened the front door and fetched water from the tap in front of the house near the creek. The tap was simple, just a piece of wood inserted into the ground. Sandra's coworker continued with his effort to rescue us. Sandra had five children. There were seven people in the house. The coworker sent his child to us to take the children to his house, one at a time.

Meanwhile, I stepped outside on the front west side of the home. I looked across the creek toward College Alfajiri and Place Mulamba. I saw people in military uniform at the Philadelphia Church. They were close enough for me to recognize who they were. They saw me and started yelling my name. I realized they were Colonel Mutebutsi's troops. I recognized their voices. We knew each other. They had been at our house before. We attended the same church. They were surprised we were still alive. They told me most Banyamulenge families had fled to Rwanda and that our family was the only one left in the Camp Sayo neighborhood. I went back inside and told Sandra.

Colonel Mutebutsi's troops at the Philadelphia Church instructed me to leave the area as fast as possible because it was dangerous for us. They said other Banyamulenge families in the neighborhood had fled, and others were killed. Some of Sandra's children had already gone to her friend's house. She was now left with only one. They went to the friend's house. I decided to go my way. Instead of going around the Camp Sayo hill, I chose to go straight across the creek toward Colonel Mutebutsi's troops, who were talking with me. I waited for Sandra to vacate the house and lock it. After she left with her kid, I began crossing the creek. This route was more challenging and dangerous because I did not know the location of General Mbuza Mabe's soldiers who were fighting Colonel Mutebutsi's troops from the hilltop. The soldiers were somewhere on the Camp Sayo hill, their gun muzzles facing toward the creek and the upper hill, where I was heading for safety. I covered myself with a towel from my head down. There were no civilians walking around in the area. I used the towel as a mask to conceal myself from other people's views.

As I began crossing the creek, I observed a male individual standing in my way on the other side. He was in his late teens or early twenties. He was facing me and appeared civilian and unarmed. The route that crossed the creek was tiny, and I did not have a way to avoid this unknown person by going around or away from him. He started whistling and facing me when I got to within a few feet of him. I took it as he was whistling to the soldiers on the Camp Sayo hill or someone else to shoot or stop me. He just whistled out loud, but he did not say a word or attack me. Because the path was so narrow, he slightly shifted to the side to let me go. I passed him, my clothes touching his. I was glad he did not try to stop or attack me.

After passing him, I climbed the small hill below the Philadelphia Church. The neighborhood did not have anybody outside wandering around. Everybody was inside their houses. It seemed like all residents in the city had abandoned it. Only birds and other noises could be heard.

When I reached Colonel Mutebutsi's troops at the Philadelphia Church, they instructed me to go to College Alfajiri, where their soldiers were resting. Though I did not see anyone between the Philadelphia Church and College Alfajiri, I was not scared because the area was under Colonel Mutebutsi's control. It was safe for me.

On my way, I saw Colonel Mutebutsi's dead soldier in the street at Place Mulamba. Second Lieutenant Mwungura was shot and died there. I knew him before he was killed. There was a roadblock in the middle of College Alfajiri. One soldier was posted there. I passed him and continued to the other side of the school premises. The rest of the troops, who were resting before returning to relieve others, were at College Alfajiri, near the Nguba Market. Captain Ndoli, one of the renowned commanders among Mutebutsi's troops, was there. Regrettably, he later died during the battle at Camp Sayo. I remember him that evening coming out of the shower with a towel. He commented, "Let me clean myself, so when I die, I die clean." His comment came back to me when I heard the bad news of his passing while fighting a few days later.

Because the Nguba district was under Colonel Mutebutsi's control, I walked from the Nguba Market to the Nguba Center, near the Congolese border with Rwanda. The majority of Banyamulenge families had fled to Rwanda. I mainly found men and young adults in the Nguba Center. Most houses were closed. Only a few civilians could be seen outside. All businesses were closed as well. The city appeared to have been evacuated.

I spent Friday night, May 28, 2004, at Nguba Center. During the night hours, I spoke over the telephone with my uncle, Pastor Zakayo Muramira, who was in the neighboring country of Rwanda. It was evident that my family had received no news about me for three days. They did not know whether I was still alive. When I spoke with my uncle, he was surprised to learn I was not dead. He urgently asked me to leave Bukavu as soon as I could. I promised I would.

I was not a soldier and did not have any business in Bukavu after escaping death two days earlier. The next morning, I crossed into Rwanda's western city of Kamembe, Cyangugu, and remained there for at least three days. My uncle and sister were in Kigali, Rwanda's capital city. But my family was still in Uvira in the Democratic Republic of Congo. Banyamulenge families in Uvira were on high alert because of the conflict in Bukavu. They feared for their lives and did not know where to go because the gunfight had turned into a conflict between members of the Banyamulenge community and the rest of the Congolese population. This was because Colonel Mutebutsi, who was fighting with his superiors and now the government, was a member of the Banyamulenge community.

I chose to go back to my family in Uvira. I could have gone to Kigali, where it was safe, but I did not. I felt the responsibility of looking after my elderly parents, especially during tough times. I left Cyangugu, Rwanda, and went to Uvira to be with the rest of my family.

I learned that hate-filled human beings are not better than wild animals. There is no difference. A dangerous animal can attack and eat a human, as a hate-filled human being can. I also learned that God's protection is beyond imagination. I felt God's presence at that time. Have you had the feeling of meeting with death face-to-face but escaping it afterward? Can you imagine getting away from armed people coming after you? Take heart when you find yourself in a life-or-death situation. Everything has an end, good or bad. But, always hope for the better.

Now that I have discussed my life experiences in Bijombo, Uvira, and Bukavu, I will take you to the United Nations refugee camp of Gatumba, Burundi, where I escaped death again when hundreds of Banyamulenge members were slaughtered and burned alive. In Chapter 3, I will explain what happened during and after the massacre against the refugees and how the survivors left Burundi and went to Western countries.

GATUMBA REFUGEE CAMP: THE GRAVE OF MY PEOPLE

*Yea, though I walk through the valley of the
shadow of death, I will fear no evil; For You are with me;
Your rod and Your staff, they comfort me.*
– Psalm 23:4 (New King James Version)

THROWING ROCKS WHILE CROSSING THE CONGO-BURUNDI BORDER

After escaping death in Bukavu, I fled briefly to Rwanda. But soon, I returned to reunite with my family in Uvira only to be forced to run again, this time to a different neighboring country, Burundi.

Banyamulenge families in Uvira were compelled to flee the city because of what had occurred in Bukavu against their relatives. Banyamulenge families in Uvira began receiving deadly threats and accusations of ethnic affiliation with Colonel Mutebutsi. The way to Burundi was life-threatening. The stay in the United Nations refugee camp of Gatumba in Burundi resulted in the loss of close to two hundred innocent refugees to armed groups from the region. Plus, over one hundred others were injured. This chapter highlights significant events leading to the massacre, what happened after the killing, and the fact that the perpetrators are known but have not been brought to justice yet.

Toward the end of June 2004, I crossed the Congo-Burundi border at the Kavimvira post into Burundi. I did not go at the same time my family did. They went to the refugee camp before me. I stayed behind in Uvira with a few of my friends. We lingered in the city because we hoped the situation would ease and those who had fled would return. Unfortunately, the situation worsened.

We stayed at someone's house for a few days until we realized the war would not stop. The few remaining soldiers from our ethnic community warned us to flee because they were fleeing as well. We rode in a vehicle from the center of Uvira to the Kavimvira border post. The ten-mile trip felt like sixty miles. We all sat in a truck bed, exposing ourselves to the public. Our faces put us at risk of getting killed at any time.

"Unload them! Kill them! Rwandans! Return to your country, Rwanda!" Thousands of people from other ethnic groups were in the streets, yelling and screaming at us as if we were thieves and deserved to die. They stopped and circled the vehicle at different locations on our way to the border. They attempted to pull off those who were sitting on the truck's edge. Those not on the edge had to hold them tight as the vehicle kept moving. Not being able to stop the truck, our attackers threw rocks at us. Some of us sustained injuries. We were fortunate that the driver did not stop for us to be taken out and killed.

I learned that when people hate others, they tend to stop seeing them as fellow humans. Killing a person comes from hating that person first. I witnessed a high level of hatred. It was imperative to request help in such a situation. Unfortunately, the Congolese government agents who were supposed to protect us played an enormous role in our persecution.

Now, let me take you inside the camp and show you how it was structured.

DIVIDED REFUGEE CAMP: THE FACILITATOR TO A TARGETED SLAUGHTERING

The town of Gatumba is located about nine miles west of Bujumbura, Burundi's capital. When we entered the United Nations refugee camp there, we quickly observed that it was divided into two parts. The camp had two sets of tents separated from each other by an empty lot. This space was later utilized to hold church services, distribute food and other materials, and conduct other minor activities, including drying clothes.

The tents on the west were white and close to the Burundi-Congo border. They were older and housed returning Burundian refugees.

Figure 3.1: The Gatumba refugee camp
The Gatumba refugee camp was structured as follows: white tents (Burundian returning refugees' section) on the Burundi-Congo border side (west side or lower left on the picture) and green tents (Banyamulenge refugees' section) on the Gatumba Center side (east side or upper right on the picture).
Illustrated by Merci Rusimbi

The green tents were newer and to the east of the white ones. They were built for Congolese refugees (mostly Banyamulenge and some Babembe families) from Uvira. A few families found shelter in the white tents because the green tents were insufficient to shelter all the Congolese refugees. Some men and youths slept outside because of the lack of space. A few other families lived in houses on the outskirts of the camp, including in the Gatumba Center. Both groups of tents were located north of the main roadway that ran between Uvira and Bujumbura. A bit farther north from the tents were toilets and bathrooms. A soccer field was in the northeast corner between the toilets, bathrooms, and the Congolese tents. Cowhouses were east of the green tents.

Two months later, the structure of the camp, with its two sides, made it easier for the killers to selectively attack only the tents occupied by the Banyamulenge refugees. The few Babembe families living with the Banyamulenge were also killed as a result of dwelling together, as the killers could not divide them at night during the attack.

Do not divide yourselves or accept being divided, as division leads to the destruction of an unwanted group. Perhaps if the camp did not have two distinct sections separated from each other, it would have been challenging, or even impossible, for regional armed groups to kill those they wanted dead. (Read about who killed the Banyamulenge refugees toward the end of this chapter.)

Speaking of separating people in order to kill the unwanted, one recent tragic example occurred on December 9, 2021, in Lueba, about ten miles south of Uvira. Joseph Kaminzobe, a member of the Banyamulenge ethnic group, had the rank of major within the Congolese armed forces. Members of the local population from another ethnic group, the Babembe, singled him out and took him out of the vehicle. He was with other soldiers from other ethnic groups. His fellow soldiers did not intervene. Major Kaminzobe was killed and burned alive in the middle of the street, surrounded by dozens of civilians. Then, his killers took a video of themselves eating his flesh. His crime? He was killed because he belonged to the Banyamulenge ethnic community. Unfortunately, the Congolese government did not prosecute Major Kaminzobe's killers.

Next, I will introduce you to camp activities. Although the refugees' everyday lives had not been restored, they continued with primary activities while they waited for the situation to ease.

DYNAMIC REFUGEES DESPITE THEIR MISERY

We had few options in the Gatumba refugee camp. We stayed there, hoping to return home soon. But unfortunately, things turned out differently than we expected. It took a long time to adjust to life in a refugee camp. Most of the Banyamulenge families in the camp had fled to the location years earlier, in 2002, but they had not stayed for long. It was a very short stay, only a few days, because the conflict ended quickly, and they returned to their homes. Unfortunately, this second time was different. The stay was longer because the battle was more complicated. In short, the situation was different from what had occurred a few years earlier. Many things happened, because we lived in the camp for nearly two months.

Most Banyamulenge were Christians. We had several churches in Uvira, and we continued practicing our religious activities in the camp. When we were in Uvira, we went to our churches in the morning. In the evening, we assembled in one big service called *igitaramo* ("A place for worship") in the biggest church structure, CADC (Communauté des Assemblées de Dieu au Congo in French, or Community of Assemblies of God in Congo). We kept the same routine inside the camp. We used the space between the white and green tents for church services. We had an early morning service called *twibature* ("Let's wake ourselves up"). Like with the *igitaramo*, members of all churches gathered in the *twibature* service. Choirs from different churches sang one at a time. After the morning service, other daily activities followed.

Another church-related activity was choir practice. Each church had at least one main choir. Most had two—one for young adults and another for children. Some churches had a women's choir. All these choirs practiced outside the camp under the trees, each at its own location. The camp did not have sufficient space for these activities because it did not have church buildings. The voices of the singers could be heard all over the camp. Some choirs practiced east of the camp, and others practiced across the roadway south of the camp. Some choirs rehearsed at night in the camp, between the two sets of tents. We were vibrant in maintaining our spiritual lives despite our circumstances.

Sport was another activity. The Banyamulenge refugees had a soccer team we called Twegerane ("Let's come together"). The team was prominent in the Gatumba area and beyond. It started and played in Uvira before its players fled the conflict. It won many games in Uvira. Twegerane played with different teams in Gatumba, especially Burundians. It won many tournaments and seemed, at one point, unbeatable, which created a hostile environment between Banyamulenge refugees and Burundians. Some of the games resulted in fighting. One day, toward the end of a playoff, a Twegerane player had the ball and was running with it, approaching the opposite team's goal at high speed. A player from the opponent (a Burundian) ran after him but could not stop him or the ball. Unable to stop him, the Burundian player punched him in the face, causing him to fall to the ground and abandon the ball. The consequences were obvious—other Twegerane players and fans stormed after the Burundian player. A few kicks and punches were exchanged among the two teams' players and fans before the fight stopped.

Only a few significant activities took place inside the camp as we continued hoping to return to our homes at any time. What we received as assistance from the United Nations High Commissioner for Refugees (UNHCR) needed to be increased. So, we began finding different ways to supply our basic needs, especially food. The Gatumba Center had casino machines, and people (natives and refugees) played the lottery. One day, I tried the lottery with one hundred Burundian francs. (I don't remember where I got it from.) Playing in the casino, I won over one thousand Burundian francs, equivalent to around thirty-five American cents today. It was not more than one American dollar back then. I brought the money to my mother, and we celebrated. She gave me about two hundred Burundian francs for my personal use. She used the rest of the money to buy our family's necessities.

Even in difficult times, you can find ways to cope with a new life and manage to survive emotional pain through daily activities you used to enjoy. I learned that it takes courage to avoid disappointment during difficult times. It takes effort to stay busy and engage in productive work while waiting for the restoration of your everyday life. If you find yourself in a similar situation, create a new routine to resume your primary activities from your old life and thrive in your new one.

VULNERABILITY TO DEATH

Back in the Congo, soldiers from the Banyamulenge community were divided and fighting on two opposing sides—one led by Colonel Jules

Mutebutsi, who was now fighting against the Kinshasa government, and another by now Lieutenant General Pacifique Masunzu, who was fighting alongside the Kinshasa government. Masunzu's soldiers were in Uvira after the city's Banyamulenge families had fled, and Mutebutsi's soldiers were fighting the country's national army in the Kamanyola area, about twenty-eight miles south of Bukavu. Most Banyamulenge refugees in the Gatumba camp favored Colonel Mutebutsi, a former brigade commander in Uvira who had gone to Bukavu as a deputy commander of the 10th regional military division. The relationship between Colonel Mutebutsi and the Banyamulenge families of Uvira (now refugees in Burundi) was tight.

Before the conflict, General Masunzu and his troops were deployed in South Kivu's high mountains about thirty miles west of Uvira. One day, a delegation of Masunzu's soldiers came to the Gatumba camp and asked the Banyamulenge families to return to their homes, claiming Uvira was peaceful. Because of a bad relationship and loss of trust in these soldiers, Banyamulenge families in the Gatumba refugee camp rejected the suggestion. They demanded that the delegation leave them alone and depart immediately. They claimed their security was not ensured in Uvira. Some male adults among the refugees became physically aggressive to the point of fighting the delegation.

It became apparent that the Congolese government encouraged several armed groups of civilians (collectively known as Mai Mai) who had taken up arms to fight members of the Banyamulenge community and force them into exile. The armed forces of the Democratic Republic of Congo (Forces Armées de la République Démocratique du Congo, FARDC) and provincial and local leaders reportedly supported the Mai Mai groups with supplies—guns, ammunition, and money—to accomplish their mission. In addition, the region was full of uncontrolled armed groups from different countries, including Rwanda and Burundi. Rwanda's Interahamwe militias, or the Democratic Forces for the Liberation of Rwanda (FDLR), which had been accused of perpetrating the genocide against the Tutsis in Rwanda in 1994, were unmanageable in Eastern Congo. Burundi's National Forces of Liberation (Forces Nationales de Libération, FNL) were also active in the region. None of these armed forces were fans of the Banyamulenge community in the African Great Lakes region. The Banyamulenge refugees in the Gatumba camp appeared to be in great, unavoidable danger of being massacred at any time.

There were many signs of a potential attack on the Banyamulenge part of the Gatumba refugee camp. Suspicious people were reportedly seen several times in the camp. These unknown people included Burundians and Congolese. Some Congolese people who traveled from Uvira to the camp were said to have come as spies. They returned to Uvira after their mission. It became evident that something terrible would happen sooner or later. Burundian security forces were in charge of guarding the camp. Two to four of them patrolled the camp every once in a while. We periodically saw them walk through the camp in the morning and at night. They hung out near the bathrooms and toilets area, west of the camp. This location was between the camp and an open, vast, unoccupied land toward Kiliba, Congo, which was on the Burundi-Congo border north of the Kavimvira post. The main Burundian security forces base was about a mile east of the Gatumba refugee camp.

My family had moved out of the camp and rented a small room nearby, a few yards away. My father's church had facilitated this because of his position in the church and because he was elderly. Several families, including mine, shared a tiny fenced-in studio complex named after its owner, Busokoza (the place was known as *kwa Busokoza*, or at the Busokoza's house). The dwelling had small single rooms with no living rooms or bedrooms. As a result, only parents and small children occupied the rooms. Inside the fenced area there was a hangar. The building was open on one side. The other side was the fence's wall. In other words, it was a hangar built in the house's fence; only a roof hung over an open space. Young adults slept in the hangar because the single rooms were insufficient for all family members. We laid out our small mattresses and slept side by side. There were about eight of us. Before going to bed, we talked about different things, including the war situation in the Congo. We also listened to various radio stations for news.

Although it was a United Nations refugee camp, it was not safe for vulnerable refugees whose enemies were within walking distance. The United Nations and the Burundian government needed a thoughtful plan to protect the Banyamulenge refugees.

Have you ever found yourself in a vulnerable position where you believed someone in authority who was responsible for your safety had betrayed you?

Now, I will walk you through the burning camp. I want to warn you about this shocking experience that still bothers me today.

AUTHORITY BETRAYAL: EXPOSED AND LEFT TO BE EXTERMINATED

Many readers may find this story unreal. It is not fiction, however. It happened, and refugees' lives were lost. Many others today bear scars on their bodies as a memory of the attack. Dozens more are crippled for the rest of their lives.

It was just like any other evening. The choirs had finished rehearsing. People had finished visiting each other—especially those, like me, who resided outside the camp—and had returned to their homes for the night. I was with my best friend, Moses, that evening. I had been inside the camp during the day. Moses and I had a place under a tree behind the Banyamulenge's tents where we spent hours writing songs. We were both choir leaders in our church. It was a cultural habit for people to walk their guests outside to their homes, so Moses walked me outside the camp to my home. We lingered along the way and spent more time than needed. We stopped several times and talked about different things. We joked about the war that was happening in our country. We joked about what would happen if we were fighting as soldiers and how we would be wounded and lose parts of our bodies. I do not know why we decided to have such an unpleasant conversation. We later realized that we had jinxed Moses because, during the camp attack, he was shot and wounded.

We said goodbye to each other after the lingering walk. Moses returned to the camp, and I went home to *kwa Busokoza*, or at the Busokoza's house. After dinner, as usual, we laid our mini mattresses in the hangar and prepared for sleep. Around ten p.m., my friends and I were discussing different things. We were also listening to a Burundian radio station from Bujumbura, Burundi's capital city. Then we heard screams and multiple kinds of noise from the camp. We also heard gunshots from the camp. Because we were used to hearing gunshots from cow thieves in the area, we first thought that was what was happening. However, the sound of weapons increased. Screams also increased; this time, there were screams of children and women. We knew something was wrong inside the camp. The sky above the camp turned cloudy and smoky a few minutes later. Then huge flames erupted. We confirmed that the camp was under a deadly attack. Because we slept in the hangar with clothes on, we did not wake up or move. We remained lying down. We were confused and did not have a place to go. Everyone was still awake at the Busokoza's house. Those inside the rooms came out. We were all in one place now, waiting for the unknown from outside. The gate was unlocked.

As we remained confused about the situation and unclear about what to expect, we heard someone push the gate violently. A woman began calling some of our names. Loud and distressed, she yelled and asked for help, saying, "*Mudutabare turashize*," or "Help us, we are finished!"

I recognized her voice. She was my sister-in-law, Aline. One of her sons, Freddy, came after her a few minutes later. At this time, the camp was entirely aflame. The whole space around the burning refugee camp was illuminated as if the electricity was lighting it up. Screams became mixed, from those of the attackers to those of the attacked. A few moments later, my cousin Dieudonne rushed into the studio complex, screaming. I recognized his voice outside the building as he screamed for help when approaching.

After about two hours, the mixed screams from the camp diminished. The gunshots stopped, and the lighting decreased. It appeared as if the attack had stopped. Then we heard marching troops in front of the Busokoza's house on the main roadway. We opened the gate to check. They were Burundian soldiers heading to the refugee camp. We left the fenced area at the Busokoza's house and followed them.

I smelled a strong odor of burning plastic materials as we approached the camp. I still remember the heavy, strange smell that polluted the air. It is not easy to describe it. I wondered if that was how death smelled. I heard cries of agony from different corners of the camp. As we approached the refugee camp from the south, we could see that only the green tents belonging to the Banyamulenge refugees were on fire. The plastic sheeting and wood were dropping to the ground in burning pieces. The white tents belonging to the Burundian repatriates were not burning. I then understood that the attackers had targeted and intended to eradicate only the Banyamulenge refugees. They killed 166 refugees and injured more than 100 others in the approximately two hours they spent in the camp, butchering with no resistance or help. Among the victims were a few members of the Babembe ethnic community who had fled the Congo with the Banyamulenge. They were killed only because the attackers could not separate them from the Banyamulenge in the darkness. Likewise, two Banyamulenge families that resided with the Burundian returning refugees were not attacked, possibly because the killers did not know they were there.

Unforgettable pictures in my mind will never leave me alone. I remember seeing dead bodies scattered all over the place as we entered the camp after the attack. The bodies of family members and friends welcomed us. I encountered Askofu's body about twenty feet east of the green tents. He was on his stomach, facing south. Askofu was the brother of my best friend, Moses. I found a family from my home village, Elias's family, in front of their tent. Elias was standing and pacing around his two daughters, Aline and Bea, with his hand on his cheek. Bea was sitting on a small stool. Her head had an open wound, and she had her head down in front of her. I realized that the wound was a bullet hole that went from one side of the head to the other. The bullet entry was near one ear, and the exit was near the other ear, creating a massive gash across her head. Aline was on the ground next to Bea. She was on her stomach and could not move. She was shot in the back. Aline's and Bea's mother and their sister had been killed while in bed inside the tent. Their half-brother was injured next to his stepmom.

I kept walking through the burning camp. The tents were full of dead bodies. Most bodies were still on fire. Some were lying in doorways, partially burned. Others had already become ashes. I could tell where a person was lying because their position remained visible in the ashes.

I walked past the last tent to the north and continued around the corner to the east, looking for survivors. Gaturuturu was lying wounded behind the tents. He could not move. Ntoni was sitting next to him with a significant wound to his head. They could communicate but were unable to move. Other casualties whose names I don't remember were next to them.

Then I heard more cries coming from the cowhouses a little farther to the east. I turned toward the voices. Dorcas and Sideriya were in what appeared to be a hole. They screamed in pain when we attempted to remove them from it. It seemed they had been hiding. They were both severely injured and were soaked in their own blood. The blankets they had covered themselves with were also soaked in blood. They were freezing and shaking. They were also thirsty and asked for water. But I knew that it was fatal to give drinking water to a person wounded by a bullet.

At this time, buses were brought into the camp to transport some of the injured to Bujumbura, Burundi's capital, for medical treatment. Family members and friends from the Banyamulenge's Ngagara refugee camp in Bujumbura had come to help us. Burundian government officials had come to assist as well. We loaded the wounded and took them to Bujumbura. Other injured refugees were taken to the medical facility in the Gatumba Center.

I made at least two rounds that night from Gatumba to Bujumbura and then back again. Some wounded refugees died on the bus during the transport. For example, during the first round to Bujumbura, I was next to Bisetsa, one of the refugees who had been shot. Bisetsa's family resided next to mine in Uvira. He was thirsty and asked for water many times. No water was around. No water was given to him. Then, unfortunately, he died halfway to Bujumbura. His father, mother, siblings, and other close family members had been slaughtered in the attack.

After transporting the wounded to the hospital, I returned and remained in the destroyed refugee camp until morning. Survivors began telling their stories, describing what they had experienced before, during, and after the massacre. One, my cousin, reported seeing and meeting the attackers before and during the attack. He had two wives. The first wife was housed in the Banyamulenge refugees' green tents, and the other was in the Burundian repatriates' white tents. Militias invaded the Banyamulenge refugees' camp when he was visiting with his wife in the Burundians' tents, which did not get attacked. He reported that he heard the militiamen and women singing church songs as they approached the targeted camp. He met them between the two sets of tents. He spoke to them in Kifuleru, a Congolese language, and told them he was one of them when they stopped him to identify who he was. They let him go as soon as they heard him speak the language, saying he belonged to them. Unfortunately, the cousin's household members, including his mother and son, were killed during the attack.

By the morning hours of August 14, 2004, the burned-to-ashes Banyamulenge refugee camp was full of people from all over the regional countries, including Burundi, Rwanda, and the Democratic Republic of Congo. They came to see what had occurred the night before. They came hoping to find their loved ones alive. Just like our experience the night before, the dead bodies of those they once called friends and family members welcomed them into the burned-down United Nations refugee camp. These new visitors wept unstoppably for their loved ones. Some even fainted and fell to the ground in panic attacks. Those strong in their emotions supported the weak. People were being carried around due to extreme emotional distress. Even Burundi's president at the time, Domitien Ndayizeye, came in the same morning with his hands to his head as he was walking around, witnessing one of the most heinous massacres in the region.

In the morning, there was a small church service next to the burned-down camp and unburied bodies. People sang church songs to comfort others. I cried uncontrollably and was comforted by someone I don't remember who was next to me. He tapped on my shoulders like I was a baby and made me believe it was okay when it was not. I stopped crying. The last time I had wept like that was when my uncle, Mukegeta, was ambushed and butchered by Mai Mai militiamen on his way home from Uvira years earlier. Unarmed, he was slaughtered due to his ethnic group, Banyamulenge, by people who knew him.

The next step was to move us, the remainder of the Banyamulenge refugees, to another location for our immediate safety. We were moved into a school in the Gatumba Center, closer to the Burundian security forces base that had failed to protect the camp. We were traumatized and could not sleep because we thought the same thing would happen at the school. A few hours later, the bodies were wrapped in plastic bags and placed in coffins, ready to be buried. The burial site, a mass grave, was near the Gatumba Center. It was an unforgettable moment.

I learned that trusting the powerful—for instance, governments and renowned international institutions—can lead to enormous disappointment when such institutions fail to do their job or live up to what people expect them to do. The United Nations and the Burundian government disappointed the Banyamulenge refugees, who had expected protection from them.

Have you ever found yourself in a situation where you could not help a helpless and innocent individual until they died? Choose to join other activists who dedicate their time and support to helping persecuted ethnic groups worldwide. Anyone discriminated against for anything deserves your support.

Now, I will shed light on the Gatumba refugee camp massacre suspects behind this cruel attack, who, unfortunately, still enjoy their freedom today.

WHO KILLED THE BANYAMULENGE REFUGEES IN GATUMBA AND WHERE IS JUSTICE?

The attackers were later identified, and the key players were suspected. They actually bragged about the act and claimed responsibility for the bloody attack on the camp.

Eyewitnesses—the survivors—reported that the attackers invaded the camp, singing church hymn songs and speaking different languages from the region, including Kibembe, Kifuleru, and Lingala from the Congo; Swahili, which is spoken in the entire region; Kirundi from Burundi; and Kinyarwanda from Rwanda. It was believed that the attackers were from different armed groups from Congo (Mai Mai groups), Burundi (the FNL), and Rwanda (the FDLR). All the groups had one thing in common: they hated the Tutsi people, including the Banyamulenge, in the region. It was also believed that some regional states, especially the Congo and its armed forces, might have played a crucial role in organizing and supporting the groups with guns and ammunition. In addition, several sources, including eyewitnesses, reported that the attackers came from and returned to the Congo.

A week later, the FNL accepted responsibility for the attack through its spokesperson, Pasteur Habimana. According to Human Rights Watch,[10] in the early morning hours after the massacre, Pasteur Habimana threatened Burundian journalists and asked them to broadcast that the Gatumba refugee camp had been attacked by Rwandan armed groups and Congolese (Mai Mai) armed groups. Human Rights Watch[11] also indicated that on August 19, 2004, six days after the massacre, members of Burundian security services arrested an FNL fighter who confessed to having killed the Banyamulenge refugees in the camp. Pasteur Habimana did not change his mind even after it became apparent that his movement

---

[10] "Burundi: The Gatumba Massacre War Crimes and Political Agendas," *Human Rights Watch Briefing Paper,* September 2004, https://www.hrw.org/reports/burundi0904.pdf.

[11] "Burundi," *Human Rights Watch Briefing Paper.*

was behind the attack and sanctions could be imposed against them. Instead, he provided a fabricated narrative, explaining the reasons his armed group had invaded the refugee camp and slaughtered unarmed refugees. Human Rights Watch and Aljazeera reported Habimana's made-up explanation on August 20 and 21, 2004.

Human Rights Watch[12] indicated that Habimana brought up unpunished killings in Burundi's conflicts between Tutsis and Hutus many decades earlier, suggesting that killing the Banyamulenge refugees was an excusable response to those unpunished decades-old Burundian massacres, as if he felt justified and that the innocent Banyamulenge refugees had to pay for what had happened or did not happen in Burundi in previous years. To him, the Banyamulenge refugees were guilty by association. Aljazeera[13] reported that Pasteur Habimana had explained their reason for attacking the refugee camp, saying that they attacked the Burundian military base at Gatumba. Then the Banyamulenge refugees assisted their Tutsi brothers, Burundian soldiers, in defeating the FNL. Pasteur Habimana continued telling his story, claiming that the Banyamulenge refugees had a headquarters inside the camp[14] and the FNL destroyed it.[15] He alleged that an attack against the Congo was underway and pretended that he was speaking on behalf of and defending the Congolese government. Habimana was neither a Congolese government spokesperson, a representative, nor a defender. He was Burundian, not Congolese, which indicates that his false claim about a potential attack against the Congo from

---

[12] "Burundi," *Human Rights Watch Briefing Paper.*
[13] "Burundi killers 'ready for tribunal,'" *Aljazeera*, August 21, 2004, https://www. aljazeera.com/news/2004/8/21/burundi-killers-ready-for-tribunal.
[14] "Burundi," *Human Rights Watch Briefing Paper.*
[15] "Burundi killers 'ready for tribunal,'" *Aljazeera.*

inside the camp was irrelevant in justifying his reason for attacking the Banyamulenge refugees.

Many credible and unbiased international organizations, including Human Rights Watch,[16] did not find evidence proving that the Banyamulenge refugees had guns inside the UN-run refugee camp. If they had been armed, the attack outcome would have been different, and some attackers might have been killed. No casualties on the side of the attackers were found in or around the camp after the attack, indicating no resistance from the refugees.

Many international human rights organizations, such as Human Rights Watch and Amnesty International, have since advocated for justice for the victims. Some heads of state also asked for an international investigation of the massacre. For example, a few hours after the killing, former South African President Thabo Mbeki[17] requested that the International Criminal Court (ICC) investigate the massacre. The Burundian government issued arrest warrants for Pasteur Habimana and FNL leader Agathon Rwasa for crimes against humanity. However, the two leaders have never been arrested or prosecuted. Instead, they—especially Agathon Rwasa—were later awarded vital positions in different governments in Burundi years after the massacre. As of today, as I write this book, Rwasa is in Burundi and has served the country's parliament in crucial leadership positions. Rwasa left the FNL and created a new political party, the National Council for Freedom (known by its French acronym, CNL). Pasteur Habimana resides in Burundi as well and has nothing to worry about. The Congolese government has done nothing to

---

[16] "Burundi," *Human Rights Watch Briefing Paper.*
[17] "Burundi killers 'ready for tribunal,'" *Aljazeera.*

seek justice for its "unwanted" citizens who were butchered overseas, just a half mile or so from its border with Burundi.

The Gatumba refugee camp survivors remain disappointed in having received no justice twenty years after the massacre. No one has ever been apprehended and tried for this bloody, heinous massacre. The incident has sent a strong signal of how the United Nations and governments, especially Burundi and the Democratic Republic of Congo, have failed to bring the suspects in such atrocities to justice. I have learned that governments' interests push them to act or fail to act in such a situation.

You can be part of the activists who dedicate their time and support to bringing to justice individuals responsible for horrific massacres, such as that at Gatumba. When governments fail to act or react, their citizens can request them to do what is right.

In the following part, I will conclude the chapter by explaining the massacre's aftermath.

AWAY FROM THE GENESIS OF BAD MEMORIES

The Gatumba refugee camp—the Banyamulenge tents only— became the ashes of both the tents and the dead bodies. One hundred and sixty-six refugees were killed, and one hundred and six others were wounded. It was now time to think about the next step. Unfortunately, going back home was not an option for numerous reasons, including the Congolese government's unwillingness to assist and welcome back the Banyamulenge refugee survivors. Additionally, the survivors themselves were disappointed and tired of their irresponsible government.

It was decided that the survivors needed to be relocated many miles away from the border. Burundi's Mwaro Province, about forty-five miles east of the Gatumba refugee camp, was chosen. The new refugee camp was built on the Gihinga hill, and the remainder of the refugees were transferred there. Before moving to the Mwaro refugee camp, we first buried our dead in one giant grave near where they were slaughtered. Several people from all regional countries attended the funeral to grieve with us. I still remember sorrowful songs by a group of Burundian supporters of the Banyamulenge refugees.

We lived in the Mwaro camp until we were flown out of Burundi to different Western nations. However, I spent more time in the country's capital city, Bujumbura, than in the refugee camp because the city offered a few opportunities, especially for youth who wanted to use their potential to build a better life, such as by attending college. On the other hand, my family lived in the camp for the remainder of our time in Burundi. I attended Hope Africa University in Bujumbura for a few months. I also led a church choir for Umoja, a refugee-based church. I visited my family in the camp whenever I could, but I was based in Bujumbura for the most part.

In April 2007, after completing the resettlement process and interviews, my family and I left Burundi for the United States. We did not apply to go to the United States. I still do not know who did it on our behalf. I did not even choose where to go in the United States. I only cared about leaving Burundi (and the entire central African region) for a better and safer country away from the genesis of my bad memories.

I learned that if the Banyamulenge refugees had been given a safe place far away from the border when they arrived at the Gatumba refugee camp and received enough security, they would not have been attacked and helplessly killed. If you are a decision-maker or an influencer in any capacity, take action for people's safety before it is too late.

In the next chapter, I will explain how I left Burundi as a political refugee and massacre survivor, then came to the United States. The following three chapters focus on my life in the United States, mainly in two cities: San Diego, California, and Abilene, Texas. San Diego is my American dream grassroots, while Abilene is the land of my most achievements to this point.

Figure 3.2: The Mwaro refugee camp
This is the Mwaro refugee camp, a site chosen to relocate the Banyamulenge survivors of the Gatumba massacre, about forty-five miles east of the Gatumba refugee camp. According to the picture setting, my family was housed in the Southwest corner.
Illustrated by Merci Rusimbi

CHAPTER 4

SAN DIEGO, CALIFORNIA: MY NEW REFUGE AND THE GRASSROOTS OF MY AMERICAN DREAM

If you spend your time hoping someone will suffer the consequences for what they did to your heart, then you're allowing them to hurt you a second time in your mind.
– Shannon L. Alder

FLYING FOR THE FIRST TIME TO THE UNKNOWN

I was one of the lucky refugees who survived the Gatumba refugee camp massacre. My family was among hundreds of Banyamulenge families who obtained immigrant visas to numerous countries in the Western world. The survivors did not apply for visas. I am still curious to know who did it on our behalf. I wonder if it was a type of compensation for our injuries and losses.

A refugee resettlement process began about two years after the attack. My parents flew to San Diego, California, in March 2007. My flight was in April 2007. My sister came shortly afterward. My oldest brother's family joined us in 2008.

The traveling process began in the Mwaro refugee camp. The survivors who were ready to travel were notified secretly by the UNHCR staff a few days before they traveled. Then they were transported to a hotel in Bujumbura, Burundi's capital city, to wait for the flight. My convoy, as we called a group of survivors who traveled together, spent about five days in the hotel. The International Organization for Migration (IOM) workers then escorted us to the airport.

Flying for the first time was intimidating, especially heading to the unknown. Besides flying for the first time, I had never been to an airport or come close to an airplane, except for a helicopter that landed in my home village, Bijombo, about twenty years earlier. Regardless of the small size of Burundi's international airport, the airport was a new environment for me. The movement and security protocol terrified me. I sat in an airplane next to my cousin Felix. We looked at each other in awe. We were speechless and did not have a way to explain our new experience. Our overwhelming state increased during the takeoff, especially when the airplane's wings tilted above the mountains of Bujumbura.

From Bujumbura, we shortly landed in Kigali, Rwanda's capital city. We remained on the plane at Rwanda's international airport. Then we met the IOM workers in Nairobi, Kenya. They were on board with us from Nairobi to New York. They helped us during mealtime and checked on us periodically during the flight.

We landed in Paris before heading to New York. When we arrived in New York, our group was divided, and we boarded different airplanes to our final destinations. The IOM workers took each one of us to our gates. They brought me to my gate, but I later realized I had missed my flight. So, they put me on another flight from New York to Denver, Colorado.

I arrived in Denver in the evening hours. I was surprised to be advised that my flight to San Diego had already left. The airplane staff advised me to sleep behind the airline counter and wait for another flight in the morning. They gave me a couple of blankets because it was cold. I told them I did not speak English, so they found me someone who spoke little French. The staff member took me to a restaurant. After eating, I returned to the counter and slept on the floor. I woke up in the morning and flew to San Diego.

I learned that the Gatumba massacre survivors were more than likely compensated for their injuries, losses, and suffering. Someone initiated the resettlement process so we could move out of the new refugee camp and to Western nations. That was how I learned to appreciate an unknown person, organization, or country. Although justice has not yet been done to prosecute the massacre perpetrators, the relocation ensured us that people cared about others and helped them as much as possible, which, as I see it, is better than nothing.

Have you ever benefited from something but had no idea who the initiator was? If so, what was your reaction? You can play a positive role in someone's life today, especially those in desperate need.

Next, I will discuss my life as a newcomer to San Diego, including my excitement and challenges and how I overcame them.

LOST BUT STRUGGLING TO FIND THE RIGHT WAY

Life in San Diego as a newcomer was tremendously challenging in a positive way. A nonimmigrant audience can't understand what immigrants go through during their first months or years of resettlement. It is a demanding experience for the better, especially for immigrants who suffered in their home countries before relocating to new nations. However, I faced challenges that could have been more pleasant. I had to overcome them to succeed as a refugee in the United States.

When I arrived, my parents had been in San Diego for a month. Despite a warm welcome from my father, mother, and their new friends, I still missed home. Nevertheless, I had to focus. I began learning about the streets of San Diego by walking around and riding a bus. Still, each morning and night felt different from home. Sometimes, I woke up thinking I was still in Africa. Almost everything in San Diego looked new to me. It felt like the Gatumba massacre had just occurred. Memories from the victims were still fresh in my mind. Memories from other survivors were still alive as well.

I bought a cellular phone. We also had a home phone. I spent countless hours day and night talking on the telephone with other survivors all over the United States and overseas. We asked each other how our trips went and how we liked our new cities, states, and countries. We shared our likes and dislikes, but the likes were enormous. We enjoyed being in developed countries. However, we agreed that we still missed home dearly, and memories of our loved ones who perished in the Gatumba refugee camp were vivid. Regardless of the distance between Africa and the United States, I kept communicating with families and friends at home via email and phone. I still do today.

Our first house was very tiny. Immigrants understand this much better. The first homes refugees get when they arrive in host countries tend to be smaller, dirtier, older, and unable to meet all the household members' basic needs. This is a general statement, not a researched finding, that I have developed after sharing experiences with numerous refugees—specifically, those in the United States.

Our first home had one bedroom, but our caseworker convinced us it was a two-bedroom house to accommodate my parents, myself, and my sister. The little house had a tiny hallway between the bedroom and the living room. Everything was small in the house, including the living room and the bedroom.

Figure 4.1: House prayer team in San Diego
When my family arrived in San Diego, California, we made friends with other refugees and formed a house prayer team that met periodically in friends' houses. My father (in orange) and mother (in white, wearing a bandana-type piece of cloth on the head) were among group members. I am sitting in front of my mother.
A prayer group team member

The caseworker placed an old mattress in the hallway and called it a second bedroom. This was my "bedroom," where I slept between my parents' room and the living room. I did not have privacy at all. I had to sleep with clothes on. If and when my parents woke up before me, they had to walk by my legs to go to the living room. This tiny hallway became my sister's bedroom when she arrived after me, and I had to sleep in our small living room. We could not live in that tiny home for a full one-year contract term. So, we complained, and the caseworker's boss came to see the house. He agreed with us and found us a better home in the same neighborhood.

The second house had two full bedrooms, a kitchen, a bigger living room, and a patio. I had to sleep in the living room because my parents and sister occupied the bedrooms. One of the couches had a bed folded in it. I unfolded the bed at night and folded it back into the couch in the morning.

I did not have a job at this time, so I could not get my own house. We all depended on the government's financial assistance through a local resettlement agency. The agency provided household items like a television, desktop computer, home phone, couches, and other basic furniture. Nearly everything in the house was used. However, we enjoyed having it, as we had come from a refugee camp where we did not have what we had in San Diego.

Figure 4.2: During the first year as a refugee in the United States
After complaining about the first tiny house that did not accommodate my entire family, this was the second house the resettlement agency found for us. I was pictured in the living room, sitting in front of the furniture provided to us through the Alliance for African Assistance.
Fidele Sebahizi

I knew my survival and growth mainly depended on my ability to communicate effectively in English. I understood language skills would open doors of opportunities that would open only with the ability to communicate in English, both speaking and in writing. For instance, I tried to apply for military service in San Diego one day. I took and failed the English and mathematics assessments. I was advised that I needed to learn more English before I could reapply. When I was growing up and going to school, French was my official language. English got very little attention in my country. Teachers taught it but needed to invest more time in it. As a result, students studied it to pass the course for a grade, but they did not hope to use it.

I needed to learn English as fast as possible. Going to college was my ultimate goal. Our refugee's financial assistance was for eight months. Then we were expected to be on our own—especially as single individuals—and provide everything for ourselves. Although I was entitled to eight months of government aid, my caseworker rushed me to find a job. He even threatened me, claiming my assistance would stop if I did not find a job as quickly as possible. I learned from a refugee friend that my aid would continue regardless of the caseworker's threats. The friend added that my caseworker's intimidation would serve only himself because he would acquire the rest of my assistance if I started working before the eight-month term was over.

It is imperative to help people help themselves by allowing them to take a proper route toward their achievement. I did not think that working without first learning English would be beneficial in the long run. So, whether the caseworker's threats about financial aid were true or not, it helped me focus on getting an English education during the assistance period. Though finding a job and making money was a good idea, I prioritized taking as many English as a Second Language (ESL) classes as possible before the end of the eighth month. Learning English was fundamental because my elderly father and mother depended on me. I was their voice. They relied on me for everything, including grocery shopping and doctor appointments.

If you are in charge of helping people, allow and encourage them to grow. Point them in the right direction. Do not interfere or be a barrier that prevents them from excelling in their lives. Please, do not be remembered badly by those under your authority and guidance (like what I am doing right now after seventeen years).

The following paragraphs explain how I learned English.

THIRSTY FOR EDUCATION IN THE NEW COUNTRY

I joined San Diego College of Continuing Education for ESL classes and attended the Mid-City Campus. Before attending English classes, I needed to take an assessment to determine my English level for placement. The Mid-City Campus had about seven different levels. The last two were intended to prepare students to transfer to a college in the city. In other words, San Diego College of Continuing Education was a system linked to the three colleges in San Diego: City College, Mesa College, and Miramar College. My ultimate goal was to go through all the ESL levels at Mid-City to transfer to one of the colleges. That is why I kept ignoring my caseworker's threats to take me out of school to find a job. I resisted until my eight months of financial assistance were over. I kept coming up with excuses to avoid him. Whether or not resisting my caseworker was a bad idea, it kept me from being a victim of education deprivation.

After the English assessment, I was placed in the same classroom, Level 1, with my father. One of the first lessons in our classroom was the English alphabet. After about three weeks, my teacher approached me and advised that she needed to move me to another level because my learning skills were faster than those of my classmates, including my father. I thought so as well. My current teacher, the next-level teacher, and the school administration agreed to move me before the semester ended. The ESL semesters were shorter than regular college semesters. So, I had less than eight months to finish all the ESL levels before the end of my financial assistance. I had to study day and evening, including weekends.

I took multiple classes throughout the day to meet my deadline. The primary topics included conversation, pronunciation, reading, and grammar. For example, one of my teachers used songs for listening lessons, such as "I Just Called to Say I Love You" by Stevie Wonder and "We Just Disagree" by Billy Dean. The songs have never left me since. Because I was thirsty for education, I took computer classes on weekends. I only took Sunday off. If the campus had offered courses on Sunday, I would have taken them.

Figure 4.3: English as a Second Language class at Mid-City, San Diego
This is my ESL class in San Diego, California, in 2007. I (wearing a white t-shirt with number 9 on it) was in one class with my father (wearing a white shirt and glasses).
Fidele Sebahizi

By the end of my assistance in November 2007, I was at Level 6+ of the ESL classes and ready to transfer to college. I had acquired enough knowledge of English and basic computer skills. This was my educational grassroots for advancing my education. I did not worry about finding a job anymore. At this point, although I still needed to learn more, I did not worry about disrupting the foundation of my education. I discovered that most refugees I knew never had a chance to find a learning institution where they could study English. I was one of the lucky ones who had found access to basic education, especially as I was over twenty years old and unqualified to enroll in high school.

You can see that you have control over your success regardless of what threatens or puts pressure on you as long as you understand what you want. If you are an immigrant, use available resources to advance quickly. Then, after advancing, you will serve yourself and your community much better. Refrain from being intimidated by present challenges and obstacles. If you are not an immigrant, you can do the same. I am sure there are plenty of resources at your disposal that you do not take advantage of. Face your challenges, and you will overcome them.

Now, let me describe my first job in the United States, which was physically demanding, had low pay, and required enormous discipline, which I had, although I needed more.

CCC: "HARD WORK, LOW PAY, MISERABLE CONDITIONS"

By the time my government aid was terminated, I had acquired enough English to express myself. So, the time had come to join the workforce. I needed more English, of course, but what I had was sufficient to introduce myself and understand what my coworkers and supervisors had to tell me. I spoke very little and was shy, fearing embarrassment. What I failed to understand was that I learned English at the age of twenty-five, which made it impossible to speak like a native speaker or even an immigrant child who had grown up in the United States. For example, my American-born children correct me every time I mispronounce an English word. Understanding that I am unable to speak like a native English speaker has comforted me over the years.

I applied for a corps member position with the California Conservation Corps (CCC). I joined the company in December 2007. At this time, I had no personal vehicle for transportation. I used a bus. Because the workplace was far from home, I took three different buses. For those who know San Diego, I lived in Mid-City but worked in National City. I had to wake up by at least four a.m. to be on time. After work, I slept on the bus home because of how tiring the job was. The work was so hard that the age requirement was between eighteen and twenty-five years old. Another interesting requirement was that employees could work for the company for only one year unless they promoted to a leadership position, which extended the term. I was almost disqualified as I was twenty-five when I joined the company. The work required enormous energy, but the pay was meager. If I remember correctly, it was five dollars and some cents per hour.

CCC's motto states, "Hard Work, Low Pay, Miserable Conditions and More!" The motto says it all. We spent hours in the sun, rain, bushes, and mountains, responding to natural and artificial disasters. Unloading sandbags from trucks was one of the activities that required muscles. We planted and trimmed trees, cleaned trails, picked up trash from the sides of highways and public parks, and performed other tasks, including preventing erosion. Almost every night, my mother applied ointment on my skin, especially my shoulders and back. This ensured the pain and soreness of the day were treated on time before it was too late.

I quickly related the job environment to my life in the Congo. Do not get me wrong—it was a tough job. However, I later appreciated the hardships I had experienced and endured in the Congo as a child. The bushes and hills where the company operated were similar to those in my home village. Evidently, childhood experience prepares us for adulthood. Who knew my misery in the Congo would serve a purpose later in my life in the United States?

What was the most challenging job in your life? What did you learn from it? Did it align with your childhood experience? Get used to reflecting on your past hardships to prepare for future ones.

Now, let me talk about how I started college. As mentioned above, the initial contract for working for the CCC was one year. However, I did not finish it for numerous reasons, especially the intense work requirement and the time I spent on the bus, which I could have used for resting if I'd had a car. Most importantly, I had found a way to begin college, which greatly motivated me to quit the job. Because I still lived with my parents, I did not have to worry about bills. I took advantage of the situation to advance in my education.

A LEAFLET THAT CHANGED MY LIFE

Going back to college was a dream come true. Looking back on my earlier years, I saw that my education had been interrupted several times, not because I wanted it to be but because of uncontrollable life events. So, I was excited to resume my education in the United

States—my dream country after my home country. I understood the United States school system would challenge me in numerous ways, but I was not ready to back down.

My thirst for education kept growing. My routine thoughts involved thinking about how to go to college. In other words, college dominated my daily thoughts at work and at home. One day, as I was reading several flyers, booklets, and pamphlets posted on the information board at the California Conservation Corps office in National City, San Diego, I came across a leaflet that advertised the City, Mesa, and Miramar Colleges in San Diego. The leaflet contained information on the Free Application for Federal Student Aid (FAFSA). A clear explanation of how to apply for FAFSA was given. The office had several leaflets for those interested in taking them. I grabbed one and brought it home that day. I read it multiple times on the bus. Next, I followed the instructions and applied when I got home that same night. I was excited to find a leaflet that later changed my life. My FAFSA application was approved, and City College contacted me. While still working for the California Conservation Corps, I went through the City College application process and was admitted. In May 2008, I quit working before the end of my one-year term and began taking summer classes at City College.

Figure 4.4: My father and mother
This picture was taken in San Diego, California, in 2010, one year before my mother passed away, during a Church of Nazarene ceremony in which they were ordained as ministers.
A church member

My first college classes were different from those taken by high school graduates. When I came to the United States, I brought my Congolese high school diploma, which enabled me to gain admission to City College. In addition, I was required to take English and mathematics assessments. The examinations were intended to test my English and mathematics knowledge and place me in suitable classes. I took English and mathematics courses below the college level. After a few semesters, I reached the standard level and started taking regular college courses. Because all three colleges in San Diego worked in one system, I took classes from all of them.

I majored in chemistry because my major in high school was biology chemistry. Though I did not have the opportunity to use a laboratory throughout my high school studies, I was stuck studying chemistry beyond the high school level. After getting admitted to City College, I decided to avoid looking for a job and instead focus on school. I wanted to have strong roots in college before finding another job. The goal was to find a job that would enable me to continue my education. That was when I joined the Able Patrol and Guard as a security officer in May 2009. With this job, I took my books and did homework during breaks and downtime. In May 2011, I obtained an associate's degree with honors (grade point average: 3.61, or 90.25 percent) from San Diego Mesa College.

Figure 4.5: San Diego Mesa College graduation, Class of 2011
In May 2011, I obtained an associate's degree with honors in chemistry at San Diego Mesa College.
Fidele Sebahizi

Opportunities leading to outstanding achievements rarely come. The FAFSA leaflet at my workplace was a blessing straight from heaven. I sometimes exaggerate when I think that the leaflet was there waiting for me. Unsurprisingly, many of my coworkers ignored the pamphlet and failed to take advantage of its content, depending on their priorities and whether they liked school or not. I learned that when an opportunity presents itself, it is wise to jump on it as soon as possible because it may last for only a while.

When opportunities come your way, please take advantage of them because they may not return. Who would like to have regrets and blame themselves for the rest of their lives because of a chance they failed to take?

In the next section, I recount the sad story of my mother's death, a life event that considerably shook me.

SMILING AT HER GRANDDAUGHTER'S PICTURE ON HER DEATHBED

Losing my mother was the most bitter life experience I have ever had. I lost her when I was attending community college and had just had my first child, Fifna.

My mother was an inspirational figure in the family. She was a strong woman physically, mentally, and emotionally. Although she had barely attended school, she provided for and sustained her family. Her ambitions involved seeing her family succeed in all aspects of life. My small achievements always pleased her. When we first arrived in the United States, she wanted me to buy a car and stop using a bus for transportation. She wanted her family to get out of poverty. That was her biggest desire of all time.

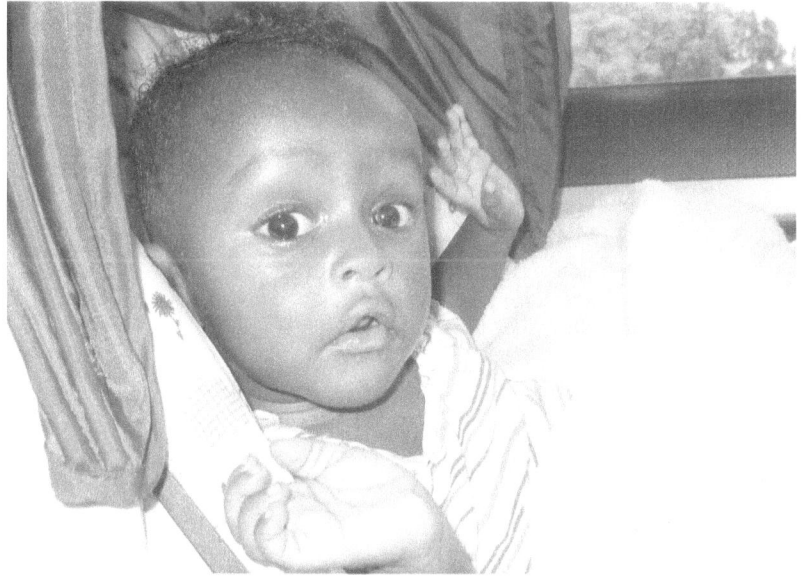

Figure 4.6: My first child, Fifna
Unfortunately, my mother and Fifna did not have a chance to meet in person. My mother met her granddaughter indirectly using a picture.
Fidele Sebahizi

She started getting sick in San Diego. She visited her doctor for the illness and was told she had a tumor on her pancreas. Nobody in the family, including herself, was aware of her sickness before we came to the United States. The only solution given was to go through surgery to remove the tumor. She did not hesitate. After the surgery, the family learned that the surgeon did not do the procedure correctly. A second surgery was unavoidable. When my mother knew about the second surgery, her facial expression changed immediately. She looked down with her hand on her cheek and pondered momentarily. She shook her head in awe. She said the second surgery worried her. "I don't think I will come back from it." She was right. She did not come back from the second surgery. The family encouraged her to go through the second surgery because we did not have an alternative.

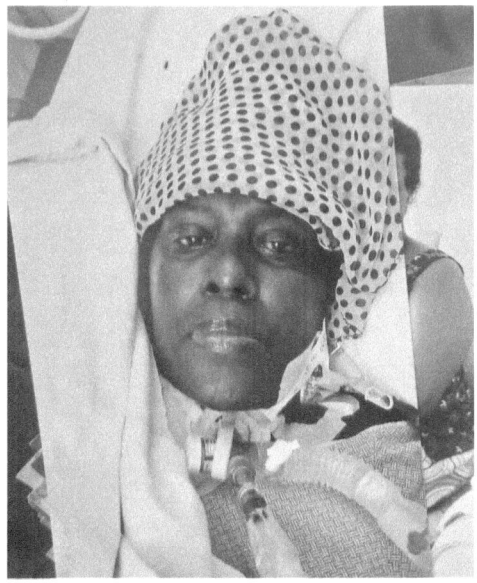

Figure 4.7: My mother in her last hours of life on her deathbed
This is one of the last pictures of my mother on her deathbed at UCSD Medical Center in San Diego.
Fidele Sebahizi

A different doctor conducted the second surgery. The second doctor's task was to repair the damage done by the first. Unfortunately, my mother died days later after the surgery. After the second surgery, she was placed on supportive machines with the hope that she would get better. She never did. She stopped communicating by voice and shook her head yes and no.

Fifna was born during the same week my mother went to the hospital. Because the hospital did not permit us to bring her to my mother's room, I showed my mother Fifna's picture when she was connected to tubes. I still remember my mother's beautiful and sad smile when she saw my daughter's picture. I also showed her a photo of my second and newer car. On March 5, 2011, my mother rested in peace after the family allowed the hospital to unhook the life support.

I learned that many circumstances are beyond human control. I wish I could have stopped my mother from dying, at least to give her time to hold my firstborn in her arms. I wish she had lived longer to witness my achievements. She would undoubtedly rejoice in my accomplishments because that is what she hoped for her family. Every time I achieve something—for instance, being a police officer or obtaining a Ph.D., I remember her and how she would have celebrated with me. If loved ones who passed away watch their family members on Earth, I am sure she watches and celebrates my achievements.

You can control only what you can control. When you cannot prevent things around you from happening, take it easy and do not stress yourself. Stress will not enable you to control what you cannot control. Take heart and move on.

The time came to take a college break because of a mental illness in my household. I will explain how it occurred in the next section.

FORCED TO INTERRUPT COLLEGE STUDIES

A mental illness in my household that had started a few months earlier forced me to take a break from attending college. It was not a choice I made. I became conditioned to the new obstacle and needed time to reorganize myself. I knew it was not the end of my educational endeavor. It was just an interruption.

My daughter, Fifna, was two years old, and her mother had a severe mental illness. I had no babysitter and could not afford to hire one. My mother, whom I had counted on for babysitting assistance, had just passed away. So, I took a short school break after college graduation to care for Fifna. Life was getting more complicated, and my income was limited. My daughter needed special attention from me as her mother could not take care of her due to her consistent mental health crisis. She stayed in mental facilities for months whenever the situation worsened. The most prolonged stay was seven months.

My family helped me. However, their help felt insufficient. I wished my mother was still alive to help even more. This was one of the burdens that forced me to take a college break. I needed to boost my earnings. Raising my income with a security officer position was impossible. I wished the security company I worked for offered more overtime hours. I quickly realized I needed another job.

I later learned that I needed the school break to reorganize myself and possibly address the problem, although it was later shown that the break did not help fix the issue. But this was not the end.

When you face a challenge, taking a step back may be necessary and reasonable before you jump back into the action. It helps relieve stress and allows you to reenergize. Please do not beat yourself up, blame yourself for anything, or think it is a defeat.

Now I will explain how, regardless of the mental illness in my household, I was employed on an oil rig in the middle of the Pacific Ocean, trying to earn more money.

LOSING EVERYTHING WHILE TRYING TO GAIN MORE

A combination of psychological and financial stresses made me quit the security job I had held for over four years. The job enabled me to attend college because I worked during evening hours, which allowed me to go to school in the morning. It also permitted me to study outside of class and do homework. Then a friend introduced me to an exciting position on an oil rig in the middle of the Pacific Ocean. It sounded like this custodial and food services position paid more than the security one. However, I later regretted my decision because it did not work out as I had thought.

I learned about Universal Sodexo Remote Sites from a friend who worked for the company and recommended I apply. The company provided facilities management and food services to multiple businesses. I completed my application at the Ventura, California, office, which was north of San Diego, about a five-hour drive. I got the job, and my assignment was offshore on an oil rig in the Pacific Ocean. When I started work, I drove to the Ventura office and parked my car. Then a helicopter flew us to the oil rig. The flight time was about fifteen minutes. We stayed there for three to four weeks, then went home for two weeks.

My primary job involved helping cooks wash dishes, cleaning, mopping, making beds, and doing laundry. I worked for the company for a few months. I later realized that the two challenges that had made me quit school still needed to be addressed. The new income still needed to be more. Spending three or four weeks on an oil rig kept me from caring for my daughter. Taking two weeks off at home required me to use all the money I had made. When I returned to the oil rig for three to four weeks, my bank account was overdrawn before I received another paycheck. I got tired of this cycle of shortcomings and decided to do something else to confront the existing, unchanging two issues.

Sometimes, it happens when you try something new to get more of what you need. You leave the one behind and pursue the other, only to realize you do not have either one. Remember that I stopped attending college to get some relief and address frustration caused by the mental illness in my family? I also quit the security job that permitted me to go to school. Then I thought the position in the Pacific Ocean would bring more relief from psychological and financial stresses. But I learned that the new position created more issues than I had expected it to solve.

Feel free to try new things. You can always change them if they do not work out as expected. You do not want to fear change only to later discover that you prevented yourself from growing by creating unnecessary boundaries.

Now, let me discuss the blessing of attending Point Loma Nazarene University to resume and advance my education.

A BLESSING THAT ENDED SUDDENLY

Although I regretted quitting my security job and interrupting my education to work on an oil rig in the Pacific Ocean, the future had better things for me. It took little time to realize that working remotely from home for a lengthy period was a bad idea. It did not fix the issues that had made me interrupt school and abandon the security job I had cherished. Instead, it created more problems. A change was warranted. I liked the idea of obtaining a job within the

San Diego city limits and being home, taking care of my family daily. I still wanted to go back to school, though.

I transitioned my work and school to the Christian-based Point Loma Nazarene University in San Diego. In October 2012, I found a gardening position at this university. The job enabled me to be psychologically and financially stable. The schedule was also helpful. I worked daily on weekdays and got off on weekends. That gave me enough time to be with my family and care for my daughter. Working for Point Loma Nazarene University was a twofold blessing. First, I worked and made money to support my family. Second, all university workers could take free college-level classes if going to school did not disturb their work. The university limited its workers in terms of how many course hours they could take each semester.

I did not want to be among those who did not use this opportunity to advance their education by taking free classes at a respected private university. I cherished the opportunity and quickly spoke with my supervisor about resuming college studies. After examining my request, my manager approved me going into the program. I began taking courses in the evening during my work schedule. Before registering for a class, I needed my supervisor's approval to ensure the class would not disrupt my work.

I decided to change majors. I had already made up my mind not to continue with chemistry at the bachelor's level. I made the decision after talking to my chemistry professor and classmates. I took almost all my chemistry classes at San Diego Mesa College and became part of the Bridges to the Baccalaureate Program, a Mesa College student program through the University of California San Diego (UCSD). The eligibility depended on academic achievement, especially a high grade point average (GPA). Those students eligible for the program had the chance to work with UCSD chemistry professors in their chemistry laboratories. It was a prestigious opportunity to be part of the program.

But even with an associate's degree with honors in chemistry from San Diego Mesa College, I switched majors at Point Loma Nazarene University. I decided to major in English—specifically, creative writing. Point Loma Nazarene University had several majors and minors to choose from. I preferred English over other majors for numerous reasons. One reason was that, as an immigrant from a country that did not speak English, I needed to advance and sharpen my English knowledge at the bachelor's level. At this point, I aimed very high. I had convinced myself to go to graduate school. However, I was still deciding what I would study. I was optimistic that English would serve me better in any program I chose. I was laying a new foundation for something much bigger than what I'd had in mind years earlier.

While taking classes at Point Loma Nazarene University, I wrote poetry, fiction, and nonfiction. At this university, I learned the anatomy of English grammar. I studied the structure of English grammar and how to break down all the parts of a sentence and their relationship to each other. It was fascinating. Unfortunately, I did not finish my bachelor's degree at Point Loma Nazarene University. I lost the opportunity to go to school free of charge because I had to move from California to Texas. San Diego had become so expensive that my income alone could not support my family. I moved from San Diego to Abilene because my brother already resided there. Though I was leaving my father and another brother behind, I could not go anywhere else because I wanted to stay close to my relatives. The next challenge would be to find a school where I could continue my college studies.

I did not give up on my educational endeavor, even if I had to work during the day and study at night. I still had to go home after work and school to care for my family, who desperately needed my presence and assistance—specifically, my daughter, Fifna. She was always in my mind when I was at work and school.

Sometimes, you must overload yourself with projects to attain your desired goals. It may sound like a dangerous idea to encourage someone to overload themselves with daily activities because people are built differently. I encourage you to push yourself toward accomplishing a goal.

In Chapter 5, I will discuss my life in Abilene, Texas. I will describe various life events, including working for the Texas Department of Criminal Justice as a correctional officer and the Abilene Police Department as a police officer. I will also explain how I continued my education until I obtained a Ph.D. while serving the Abilene community as a police officer.

ABILENE, TEXAS: THE STEPPING STONE TO VICTORY

We think about education as a stepping stone into a higher socio-economic class, into a better job. And it does do those things. But I don't think that's what it really is. I experienced it as getting access to different ideas and perspectives and using them to construct my own mind.
– Tara Westover

THE TWENTY-HOUR ROAD TRIP LEADING TO SUCCESS

San Diego, California, became too expensive for me. I worked alone in my household and needed to move to a place where the cost of living was affordable and I could support my family. At the same time, I needed to move to where my oldest brother lived so we could stay together, although my father and my other siblings lived in several cities and countries.

In the summer of 2015, I fueled up my 2010 Chevrolet Impala and drove from San Diego, California, to Abilene, Texas, with my daughter, Fifna, and her mother. The twenty-or-so-hour trip was unpleasant with a small car full of household belongings. Fifna was sitting in the back, taking one seat, while the other two were used for household items. Even the front passenger seat floorboard contained minor things because I could not find room in the back seat or trunk. Thankfully, I experienced no issues on the journey. If I had, I would not have been able to afford other costs beyond food and gas. I had no money for the inconvenience.

Around seven p.m., I hit the streets of a small town (compared to San Diego) called Abilene. The roads appeared empty. It was my second time being there. For Fifna and her mother, this was their first time. They could not believe that I had brought them there. Unfortunately, they did not have a choice, nor did I. I was the family's decision-maker, so they believed in my decision-making capacity. When I arrived in Abilene, I stayed with my brother's family for a few months until I found a job because I had no money to rent a house.

When things do not work out as expected, consider changing your course of action toward a new direction. It is better to change than to stay the course with difficulties that need to be addressed. Are you stuck where you genuinely think you have to make changes? Now is the right time to decide.

The following sections will explain how I established my life in Abilene, starting with joining the state's corrections department.

BREAKING THE CYCLE

When I arrived in Abilene, I was picky about where I wanted to work. I needed to make sure the types of work I desired were available. I wanted to avoid a job where I would not be happy investing my time and acquiring new and needed skills. I wanted to develop a stable career in the years to come. At this time, I was still undecided about what my job path would be. But I had decided on the types of work I did not want.

I found many families from my ethnic group in Abilene—specifically, families we had lived with in the Congo. I was told about their different jobs and was encouraged to apply at their workplaces. I was advised to look for a job at a cookie factory and at companies that cared for people with disabilities. While the cookie factory was self-explanatory, the other companies cared for seniors. I applied at one of the companies but did not work for it because I had put in another application with the Texas Department of Criminal Justice (TDCJ) for a correctional officer position. While dealing with the first application, I received mail from TDCJ that my application had been approved and that I needed to complete specific tasks to complete the application process. I abandoned the first application and focused on the TDCJ application. I liked TDCJ better than the other jobs because I wanted to do something different from what members of my immigrant community were doing—working at one or two places throughout the city. I broke the cycle of not expanding the potential among my people when congregating at one workplace. In other words, I needed to challenge myself by going beyond my people's norm.

We all have things we want. But sometimes, we get stuck with things we do not want. People tend to follow others mindlessly and end up doing what they do not like to do. Peer pressure works. When you get stuck in the middle of two choices, pick the one that aligns with your values regardless of what it takes to reach it or what others think about it.

In the following paragraphs, I will discuss how I joined the Texas Department of Criminal Justice, regardless of what it took.

ACCEPTING MORE CHALLENGING EXPERIENCES

Getting what you want sometimes requires more hard work and sacrifice. By sacrifice, I mean letting go of the dear and pursuing the more precious regardless of the effort required. Joining the Texas Department of Criminal Justice in its corrections department appeared appealing, and I already had a sense of a potential long-term career.

I followed up with my TDCJ application by completing the steps needed to begin a pre-service training program. In the summer of 2015, I took a written test at the Price Daniel Unit in Snyder, Texas. I successfully passed the test on the same day with the assurance that I would work for an agency whose uniform I was excited to wear. After all the required steps were completed in August 2015, I started the pre-service training academy at the John Middleton Unit in Abilene. The academy was intimidating because of its rules, which were similar to military discipline. I liked what we had to go through during the academy and afterward. The rules differed from the regular world's, and I enjoyed following them. I was later convinced this was the profession I was created for. It became apparent law enforcement was my proper career.

The academy was manageable. One thing that hit me the most and left me with a strong memory was the exposure to a chemical agent (2-chlorobenzylidene malononitrile, or CS gas) known for causing burning sensations in the respiratory system. Thankfully, the exposure occurred outside in the wind. Our instructor ordered us to make four lines and tightly intertwine each other's arms. We were also required to stay together during the exposure. After a couple of CS canisters were launched in our midst, covering us in white gas smoke, we eventually ignored or forgot the instructions, and we scattered in the field, coughing with crying eyes. I thought I would stop breathing and die. But the instruction was to breathe to allow the air into our nostrils and mouths.

After more than five weeks, our class graduated, then did more than one hundred hours of on-the-job training (OJT) at the John Middleton and French Robertson Units in Abilene. I was assigned to the Robertson Unit's general population (commonly referred to as GP), as this unit was my first choice on the application. The term "general population" referred to the less dangerous section of a prison. The job was more challenging than the academy. During the academy, the cadets were briefly exposed to the inmate population during lunch breaks and training-related tours. During the exposure to the inmate population, we appeared very intimidated in front of prisoners. I thought the inmates looked at us as if we were the new invaders of their territory—the prison. Their stares were frightening, but they also scared us by insulting us as we passed by, always in a single line from and to chow (prison slang for "prison meal"). I asked myself several times, doubting myself, if I was ready to do the job—specifically, in the middle of dozens of inmates in enclosed break rooms, where offenders sat and watched television regularly.

Figure 5.1: Texas Department of Criminal Justice Correctional Officer graduation
On September 18, 2015, I graduated from the Texas Department of Criminal Justice Correctional Officer pre-service academy at the John Middleton Unit in Abilene, Texas. *Unknown*

The general population units housed offenders whose conduct was deemed good. This section comprised about seven buildings, but four were designated for rookies because they were more manageable and considered to have less aggressive inmates than others. Within the first months of employment, I worked the four buildings, switching them based on where my supervisor wanted me to work on a particular day. Besides working the four buildings, I was sometimes assigned to chow, which meant I helped feed inmates. Assignments were different in the buildings, including a desk (to coordinate all the wings inside and outside the building), a picket inside each wing (to coordinate the rover on the floor, a desk at the building entrance, and supervisors and others outside the building), and a rover (in charge of the floor inside a wing). I worked all these positions. After I had gotten enough experience, I was assigned to other buildings in the GP—those that housed inmates who were classified as more aggressive and dangerous than the rest of the GP but less dangerous than those in the segregation section (a prison within a prison).

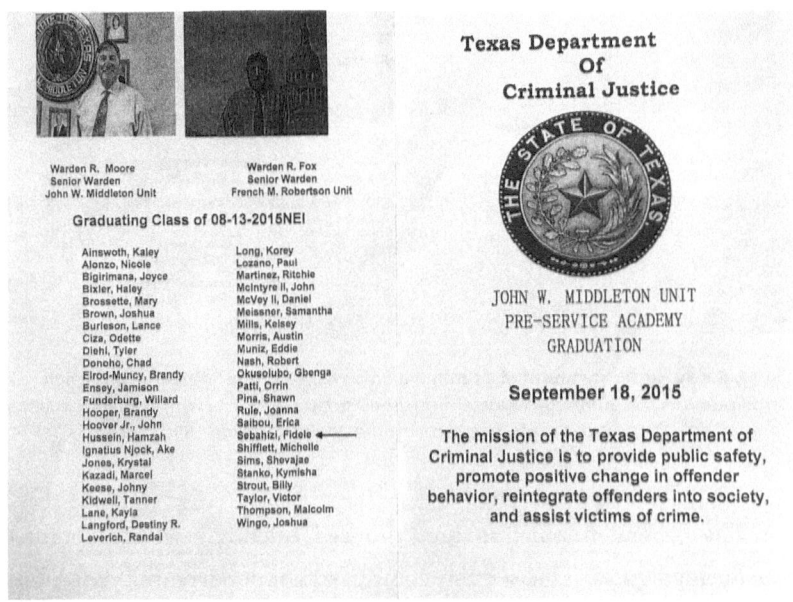

Figure 5.2: Texas Department of Criminal Justice graduation program
This was the graduation program for the Texas Department of Criminal Justice Correctional Officer pre-service academy at the John Middleton Unit in Abilene, Texas.
Fidele Sebahizi

When I arrived in Abilene, I could have chosen to care for people with disabilities and seniors, which would not have required me to endure the pain of chemical exposure and other strict, military-like rules. However, I took the TDCJ training because that is what I wanted: a more challenging experience. I later learned that the training had prepared me for similar but advanced training at the Abilene police academy, which I will explain later in this chapter.

Do not get intimidated by facing challenges in your life. Challenges help people grow.

Now, let me explain what happened with my education after relocating to Texas.

THE SEARCH THAT KEPT ME GOING

Although I temporarily stopped my education when I left California, I did not stop finding ways to resume it. Education was in my veins, and I could not ignore its calling. It was as if something or someone unseen was pushing me to pursue higher education. I had to listen.

When I arrived in Abilene, I did not wait to apply at Abilene Christian University (ACU), and within days, I was admitted. However, working as a correctional officer for the Texas Department of Criminal Justice prevented me from taking classes during the day. The TDCJ schedule was not flexible. I was required to work four days and take the following four days off. The schedule changed workdays and off days. This alternating schedule made me cancel my admission at ACU. I was not ready to quit the new job that I was passionate about.

Although I was not pleased to miss the opportunity to attend a private and well-respected Christian school like ACU, my thirst for education was not quenched. I continued searching for another institution that could give me the flexible hours I needed to keep my job. After an exhaustive search on Google, I found Southern New Hampshire University (SNHU). I was delighted to continue working on a bachelor's degree program in English, which I had started at Point Loma Nazarene University in San Diego. I began taking classes at SNHU but had to stop later to attend the Abilene police academy. Later in the chapter, I will explain how the police academy required my full attention because it was difficult. I resumed college studies after graduating from the police academy in the summer of 2017.

Abandoning school entirely had never been an option in my life, despite all the obstacles I encountered in pursuing an education. I later realized I was designed for higher education. In the long run, I learned that fighting against the little voice within me about going to school was impossible. Education was always at the top of my priority list.

It would be best to learn how to prioritize things in your life. Life is always busy and full of unnecessary things. After you understand your priorities, ensure you do not give up on them by distracting yourself.

Next, I will recount my story of working inside prison walls and how prisoners perceived and treated me, which guided me in the direction of my current profession.

CALLED A COP BEFORE BECOMING A COP

I did not play games with offenders when the Texas Department of Criminal Justice employed me. I ensured prison rules were respected at all times where I was assigned. Enforcing rules can be done without personal negative consequences for the committed enforcer only if all rule enforcers do the job without deviation, meaning being honest about enforcing the rules.

It did not take long for offenders to start calling me a cop inside prison walls. I realized they labeled me a cop because they complained I was too strict and did not give them chances to get away with breaking prison rules. Grievances grew among prisoners against me. Whenever a shift change occurred, inmates would pay special attention to incoming correctional officers. They knew who enforced the rules without deviation and who did not.

Checking incoming officers on every shift dictated how inmates behaved—whether they stayed out of trouble or engaged freely in unauthorized transactions among themselves. Those who wanted to break prison rules did not appreciate my presence in their wings or break rooms during my shift. Most of them told me in my face that they hated seeing me in their buildings. I paid no attention to it because I was doing what I was trained to do. Regardless of potential danger, I was dedicated to performing my job as I was taught because I had signed up to work in a dangerous environment. I kept my confidence high despite the possibility of an attack.

Doing the right thing when others don't can set you apart from them, causing those who feel oppressed by your way of doing your job correctly to hate you. Always do the right thing despite the potential high cost. It will pay off in the end.

In the following paragraphs, I will explain how doing the right thing got me hated and in trouble, including being physically attacked by a prisoner.

"YOU ARE AN AFRICAN BROUGHT IN MODERN SLAVERY"

Doing the right thing almost got me hurt. When I was employed in the Robertson Unit, inmates threatened me in different ways.

The threats were personal, and I related them to my strict way of enforcing prison rules. I could be wrong, and there may be other reasons I was not aware of. But my experience with offenders was the only reference point I had at that time that allows me to draw such a conclusion.

One day, a Black inmate challenged me on the second floor of the housing area when I was doing a routine count. He approached and provoked me, arguing that I was not an American. It was not the first time I was insulted, but this time was worse. The offender said it confidently and purposely because of my foreign accent. The argument was on as he aggressively followed me. He made several comments, but one stuck out: "You are an African who had been brought to the United States in modern slavery." He accused me of working for White people. As I kept walking away from him, minding my own business, he stopped following me. I was lucky that day he did not physically attack me.

Another Black prisoner physically attacked me one morning in the break room. I had worked overnight and was in the last hour of the shift. Offenders had finished eating breakfast. They ate breakfast in a building away from their residential areas. I was in charge of the floor, ensuring all inmates returned to their cells after the meal. I had to escort them into their cells and lock the doors. The inmate lingered in the break room and did not want to go to his cell. Typically, when I entered the wing's break room, the main door shut behind me. This door was controlled by a picket officer who looked down into the break room from a small, secure, elevated room.

I approached the inmate to give him an order to vacate the break room. He was the only remaining offender outside the cells in the break room. He had wrapped his right fist with a white cloth and kept bumping the wrapped fist into his left palm, indicating he was getting ready for a fight. He stood up and began pacing around in the break room. At this time, I realized I was in danger, and my adrenaline started rushing. The inmate's back faced the main entrance, making it difficult for me to escape. I attempted to communicate the problem over the radio but could not get the message out because the offender's behavior disrupted me. He charged me.

Fortunately, my picket officer had already observed the matter and called out for assistance. I had my pepper spray out and was ready to use it for self-defense. The inmate did not care about the pepper spray. He then swung at me once but missed. I sprayed him in the face. The chemical agent hit me back in the face, making us both contaminated. The offender immediately ran back away from me. Several officers rushed into the break room to my assistance. The offender was placed in handcuffs, decontaminated, and escorted to the segregation section. I headed to the medical facility in the prison to get checked out and decontaminated.

As mentioned above, I concluded that the two incidents were most likely related to how I enforced rules in the prison. Because I abided by the prison rules and felt the obligation to implement them as they were, it almost got me hurt or killed. The two offenders were among those who were displeased by how I enforced the prison rules.

While I do not recommend that you get hurt purposely to be a hero, I encourage you to do the right thing and ensure your safety.

Now, let me explain how I became a real cop on public streets, not in prison walls, as offenders had anticipated.

THE TRIGGER OF THE CALLING FOR BECOMING A REAL COP

Working in prison as a correctional officer became a sign that I was made for something similar but different from my assignment there. Although there was potential for me to be promoted, offenders saw and confirmed something in me that later pushed me out of working in the prison.

Many offenders suggested I join the Abilene Police Department. It is unknown if the suggestion was based on their hatred of how strictly I enforced prison rules or if they genuinely thought I was a good fit for the police. They argued that prison work was not for me. They said I was harsh on them, explaining they were home and wanted to run the prison the way they wanted because some of them were there for life. However, prison rules were there for a reason, and inmates were expected to obey them regardless of their wishes. They also argued that other officers were lenient with them, enabling them to do drugs and other bad things. As a result of my stance regarding enforcing prison rules the way they were designed, offenders filed countless grievances against me with no negative impact on me because I was doing the right thing, which illustrated one of the four Texas Department of Criminal Justice core values: integrity.

In April 2016, my supervisory team selected me to become a mentor in the on-the-job training (OJT) program. My primary responsibility was to train new officers upon graduation. The offenders' suggestion that I join the police force had become a seed planted within me, and it was germinating. Coupled with the fact that I needed to grow more by pursuing other similar professional careers, I kept thinking about joining the police department in Abilene. Whether the inmates' recommendation was genuine or not, I had a conviction that I would do everything possible to become a police officer.

Sometimes, it takes other people to help you discover your potential and inform you what you can do for others. You can learn who you are from others, including those who may consider you their enemy, as it turned out for me at the French Robertson Unit. When people tell you what they see in you, please do not ignore them. Others can easily see your true self, but lying to yourself about who you think you are is effortless and pointless.

The following section will explain how I joined the Abilene Police Department.

THE LITTLE VOICE THAT LED ME TO VICTORY

Sometimes, significant changes in people's lives happen instantly. A turning point toward a massive movement in someone's life can take only seconds. I did not expect how things turned out that day. It was a typical day, and I was not thinking about a big change in my life.

In April 2016, I visited the Abilene Police Department station to inquire about a legal matter. It seemed as if I heard a voice within me instructing me to contact the police recruitment office for information on how to apply. Without hesitation, I asked how to get ahold of a recruiter. I immediately emailed the recruiter. The recruiter advised that the 2016 application deadline was approaching fast, and my inquiry had arrived just in time. When I got home from the police station, I filled out the online application. The beginning of the application process was exciting. My supervisor and coworkers at the French Robertson Unit learned about the process and wished me success.

I did not ignore that little voice I heard that day. It was a sharp turning point toward a new endeavor I had never imagined. I still cannot comprehend how it happened that quickly. All I did was obey the voice.

Have you heard of that little voice and purposely ignored it? Have you wondered what would happen if you listened to it? People miss opportunities when they avoid small indications that lead to bigger things. The little voice comes every time. Do not miss or ignore it again.

Let me tell you about my divine dreams during that time, which confirmed I had a calling to become a police officer.

THE DIVINE DREAMS CONFIRMING MY PATH TO BECOMING A POLICE OFFICER

Dreams occur unintentionally during sleep. Some are remembered, while others are not. Some people's dreams come true, but many do not. I am a believer in Jesus Christ. I believe in divine authority and the will of God. I have had several divine dreams that confirmed that I was on the right path to becoming a police officer, no matter the challenges I faced.

On March 20, 2016, I saw myself in a dream taking a test similar to a school exam. Two or three people asked me different questions. I saw myself excel, and my performance was approved. Those who were questioning me were amazed. I understood the dream's meaning only when I went through the application process and was in the police academy. For example, during the oral interview board toward the end of the process, recruits had to sit in front of a team of police officers and city civilian employees to explain why they wanted to join the police force, answer questions, and do practical scenarios to show they could do the police work. My performance was admirable, and I passed.

On April 28, 2016, I had a more specific dream about the police academy. I saw myself in a police academy, ready to begin the training. It appeared I had found others already at the training site. Still in the dream, I saw two young Banyamulenge (my ethnic group) men and realized I did not know they had applied. I dreamed of the three of us discussing similar training in Africa—specifically, how cadets would endure hardships on the first day, such as rolling around in the mud. This dream was fulfilled on the first day of the academy. However, the two young Banyamulenge men I saw in the dream were interpreted to be two American-born Black cadets I later met in the academy. Different from what I dreamed of in the second part of the dream, we did not talk about training challenges in Africa because they were not from Africa.

On December 6, 2016, when I was about to complete the application process, I had another dream. The dream was obvious and exciting in how part of it was fulfilled the following day. I dreamed of a few people wearing light-blue uniforms and marching in a single line before me. I told one of them that they were wearing a uniform similar to what we wore in the police academy. At this time, I had not started the training and did not know what color of uniform Abilene police cadets wore in the academy. The following day, I received a phone call from the Abilene police academy, instructing me to go downtown to a uniform store for uniform measurement. Interestingly, the uniform was light blue, matching the color in the dream.

On February 15, 2017, I dreamed I had finished the police training and was walking in the middle of a roadway and wearing the regular dark-blue police uniform. The uniform did not look ironed, and it appeared I had not acquired enough policing experience. In the dream, I looked like a rookie.

On a different day, which I did not recall or record, I dreamed of communicating on a police radio. During the dream, my first radio traffic was unclear to the person I was speaking with. But my message was clear when I said it for the second time. In the dream, I saw myself communicating with no hesitation or nervousness. These dreams were later fulfilled. Upon graduating, I wore the regular dark-blue police uniform. I was a rookie for months, learning how to police in real life on the streets. Because of my heavy accent, dispatch communicators had issues understanding me on the radio. They still do to this day because my accent has not gone anywhere.

You may not believe in dreams. You may have dreamed, but your dreams never came true. Regardless, I am living, breathing evidence that some dreams come true. I write down dreams that stand out and revisit them occasionally to see if they have been fulfilled. If you believe in supernatural powers, you may start paying attention to your dreams for guidance, especially when you are uncertain.

Next, I will describe the details of the basic police training at the Abilene police academy—especially how I overcame obstacles.

POLICE ACADEMY: CHALLENGED BUT REFUSED TO QUIT

The endurance required in a police academy can be understood only by people who have experienced it or been in similar training settings. One of the most intimidating days was the boxing day. The days we were exposed to chemical agents and the Taser were also challenging.

Some of the recommendations the academy staff gave us before basic training included physical exercise, such as running and doing push-ups and sit-ups regularly. Another suggestion was to put regular schooling on hold until the police training was complete because the academic portion of the training was difficult. I did what was recommended to ensure I was fit for the training. I ran and did push-ups and sit-ups almost daily. I did most push-ups and sit-ups on my breaks and during downtime at the Robertson Unit, primarily when I was assigned to work in the picket. Unfortunately, I learned in police training that my style of push-ups needed to be corrected. I realized my push-ups were not complete and accurate, meaning I needed to stretch my arms all the way up and go all the way down. I learned about this on the first training day.

Figure 5.3: Police academy cadet binder
This was one of my police academy binders during my 2017 police training in Abilene, Texas.
Fidele Sebahizi

The first day of physical exercises was very intimidating and intense. I almost fainted after running and doing many push-ups, sit-ups, and other exercises for a long time. I had to sit down and be evaluated medically, including checks of my vitals. But I had determination. I was determined enough to tell myself I would not give up even if an ambulance had to take me to a hospital. This mindset has served me best to this very day. Quitting was not an option. At this time, I was taking college classes for my bachelor's degree at Southern New Hampshire University. But I had to put my schooling on hold to focus on the police academy. I resumed my college studies after graduation.

I had several challenges throughout the police academy that I could have used as excuses to quit. They were legitimate enough to convince almost everyone. However, I had to overcome them regardless of how difficult they were. I will discuss only a few. I will begin with what I consider the simplest of all, meaning what all my classmates in the police academy underwent. The legitimacy of the challenges is specific to what I experienced outside the training. The obstacles I encountered at home could have prevented me from completing the academy. Friends told me later they did not understand how I managed the police academy and a mental health problem in my household.

The boxing day was an enormous trial for me. Entering the boxing ring gave me goosebumps. All the cadets signed a liability form, the phrasing of which I do not recall. But I understood when I signed it that I acknowledged that I was responsible for anything that happened to me while boxing. The boxing ring was small and in a half-dark room. Regardless of its size, it was scary, but the mindset of not quitting kept growing even more robust. The boxing was not open to the public. Only authorized personnel—specifically, the academy staff and volunteers from the police department—were allowed to attend. All the cadets were matched based on their sizes. Each had to do three rounds of boxing. Waiting for my turn was a killer. It felt like I had cold water in my stomach. My hands were freezing, but my determination was not, even after I saw others knocked out.

When my first round was up, my name was called out. I put on a helmet and gloves. Some of my classmates began chanting, "Go, Seb!" "Seb" had become my nickname at the beginning of the academy because my last name was unique and difficult to pronounce, and many found it challenging to say it. When I worked for the Texas Department of Criminal Justice as a correctional officer, prisoners found my last name hard to say as well. They nicknamed me "Easy" for "Izi," the last three letters of my last name.

I do not remember how long the first round lasted, but I think it was one minute. However, it felt like it lasted for an hour. I lost the fight. There was one punch that made my head shake. Once the bell rang, I felt relieved, but the battle was not over because I still had to fight two more rounds with two different people. I had no idea who they were. It was a surprise. I was dizzy at this time but not ready to quit. For the second and third rounds, the fight time was increased. I won the second round. During the third round, I lost the fight again.

The academic portion of the training was demanding. We learned different Texas codes, including penal, transportation, family, and criminal procedure. Physical exercises were tiring and increased in intensity every day. Except for the first day of the academy, when I almost passed out, I did not have issues running for the rest of the training. I was among the first two cadets to finish each running section. The day we ran six miles for the badge, I finished first.

The Taser day was intimidating. Officers kept joking with the cadets and reminding them about the Taser day when all cadets were scheduled to be tased. I was curious and nervous about how the Taser worked in the body. The day came, and all the cadets were placed in one room to be tased one at a time. Afterward, it was impossible to describe how it felt. But to me, it felt like an enormous heavy item, such as a house, being placed on my back. The five-second cycle felt like an hour of pain.

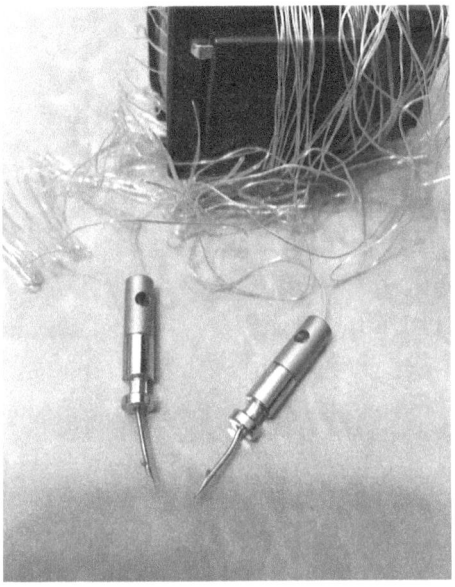

Figure 5.4: Used Taser probes on me
This picture shows the Taser probes used on me on the day we were tased during our police academy.
Fidele Sebahizi

The training was eventful on the days of chemical agent exposure to 2-chlorobenzylidene malononitrile (CS) and oleoresin capsicum (OC), commonly known as pepper spray. I had been exposed to CS gas in the

Texas Department of Criminal Justice training. Still, this second exposure in the Abilene Police Department training felt totally different. The drill occurred in a small fire department training building with two tiny, dark rooms. We were placed in one room, while CS canisters were exploded in another. We were placed in a line, hands together, and instructed to walk into the gassed room and out the front door. We lost control once we were in the room with gas smoke. I was confused to the point of missing the way to the front door. I attempted to return to the room with CS canisters, but another cadet pulled me outside the building.

On the other hand, the OC exposure occurred outside. An instructor sprayed us in the face. Before accessing the water hose, we had to perform physical drills, such as punching, kneeing, and elbowing at different stations. The gas exposure was so intense in my eyes that I almost called my brother to come to pick me up from the training site.

As expected from a trainee, I made several mistakes throughout the academy. However, one mistake sticks out in my memory to this day; it helped me prevent potential, dangerous future mistakes. One day, during practical exercises of a high-risk traffic stop, I made a colossal error that needed to be addressed in a particular way. The exercise was about handling firearms in a team movement. One specific area that needed special attention was avoiding cross fire. We trained with rubber guns with live training ammunition. But with the seriousness of the training, we treated the rubber guns like real firearms with ammunition. Any mistakes with them were considered done with live guns and bullets. I made an error by pointing my rubber handgun at another cadet, which I did not know until one of the instructors called it out. It was during the drill in which I approached a parked vehicle alongside other cadets in a moving formation. I must have stayed a little behind for my muzzle to point at another cadet. As a result of such a fatal mistake, I was ordered to run about a half mile with my gear on. I was embarrassed, but the punishment was needed to prevent future errors.

Our police academy Class 54 began on January 9, 2017. We were twenty-one police cadets on the first day of the academy, and only fourteen graduated on July 27, 2017, after twenty-nine weeks of intensive physical, academic, mental, and emotional training. I later learned that Class 54's applicant pool was 141. This means 120 applicants did not make it to the first day of the training for numerous reasons.

I became the first immigrant to join and work for the Abilene Police Department and the first member of the Congolese Banyamulenge ethnic group to become a police officer in the United States.

Figure 5.5: Abilene Police Academy graduation day
On July 27, 2017, I graduated from the Abilene Police Department Academy (Class #54).
Chris Mwungura

Endurance requires determination. Because quitting was not an option, the challenges I went through did not intimidate me to the point of giving up. The training was physically, academically, psychologically, and emotionally demanding, but I kept a positive attitude until graduation.

Before you think about facing an obstacle, your first step is determining what you want beyond such an obstacle. If what you want is worth the pain, go for it, and you will conquer.

The following paragraphs will underline a family struggle I had to overcome on top of challenging police training.

Figure 5.6: Abilene Police Academy graduation day
Here, I was looking forward to the second training phase, on-the-job training or applying the law.
Chris Mwungura

OVERCOMING A MENTAL HEALTH CHALLENGE DURING THE POLICE ACADEMY

Besides the police training challenges, I encountered another inevitable issue I had to overcome. It was a mental illness in my household that had not stopped but presented itself as a barrier to keeping me from joining the police force. It was a burden that weighed heavily on my shoulders.

I still had one child, Fifna, when I joined the Abilene police academy. Fifna's sister, Faith, was born after the police academy graduation and during the on-the-job training. A member of my household I wish not to disclose here for personal reasons went through several mental illness episodes during this period. I will call her Daniella to protect her identity. When I was still going through the application process in 2016, Daniella was in a very concerning mental health crisis. Nevertheless, I did not have enough courage to abandon the process. I persisted and did not let go. That was when I realized, and am still convinced, that God was pushing me toward something very significant. The mental health crisis worsened enough that Daniella stayed in local facilities for weeks. One time, she spent seven months in a state-run mental health facility out of town. I had to deal with this and care for Fifna, who was now six years old. My family helped me as much as possible, including having my daughter stay in their homes.

One day, during the first months of the police application process, I drove to Kentucky from Texas and returned the following day. Daniella had been discharged from a mental health hospital. She did not want to stay home or anywhere else with my family. She preferred to go be with one of her own family members. The week I transported her to Kentucky, I had an appointment for one of the tests I needed for my application. The appointment was very significant for the process, and if I missed it, I would not be considered for the 2017 academy. I had to address the mental health crisis during that week and come back to Texas for the following week's scheduled test. I left Fifna in my brother's house and drove more than thirty hours from Texas to Kentucky and back.

On my way back to Texas the following day, Daniella's other family in Kentucky called me and advised that she had become more of a problem. They wanted me to go back and get her because she was my responsibility. I told them my scheduled test was approaching fast, and I could not drive back to get her and make it to the appointment. I did not want to risk missing my scheduled test. I asked the Kentucky family to be patient and wait until I finished the assessment. The following day after the appointment, I drove back to Kentucky and brought Daniella home.

The application process and the police academy continued regardless of my need to deal with the mental health illness in my household. For example, one day, when I returned home from training in the evening, I found that Daniella had put several household items outside in the side yard alongside the main roadway. I brought everything back into the house. She continued misbehaving that night because she was in a mental health crisis. She became physically aggressive toward me to the point that I locked myself inside my bedroom. I worried about my safety. I did not want to get hurt while asleep. However, Daniella broke the bedroom door with kitchen knives. Fortunately, she did this while I was still awake. I left my residence and found a place to sleep for a few nights. I took only training equipment with me and left everything else behind. My daughter, Fifna, was at my brother's house during this time.

The behavior was prolonged the following days. One day, when I came home from training, the situation worsened. At this time, I had to call the police for assistance. While police officers investigated, unfortunately, Daniella followed me into the kitchen area and slapped me in the face once. The slap did not hurt. But because she did it in front of the police officers, they had to arrest her. I told police officers that the slap did not hurt, and I did not want to pursue charges against her. However, they still arrested her because Texas domestic violence law required them to do so.

Figure 5.7: My second child, Faith
Faith was born in 2017 while attending the on-the-job phase of the Abilene Police Department academy.
Fidele Sebahizi

Regardless of the difficulty of dealing with mental health problems in my household, I did not quit the police academy. I pressed on, although the burden was heavy. I had homework to do, and dealing with an uncontrolled mental health patient at home and doing homework was not a good combination. One night, when I was doing homework, I thought about what I was going through until I had a heavy headache. I did not want to kill myself, but I was hurt enough that I felt I needed something to calm myself down. I thought about different things that could help. I did not drink at that time, and I still do not drink today. But I then decided to buy alcohol. I went to a nearby convenience store and bought a six-pack of an alcoholic beverage. I did not pay too much attention to the brand. All I wanted was to get drunk that night to help with my thoughts and sleep.

I was by myself in the living room when I opened the pack. I took about three sips, then I changed my mind. It is as if I heard a voice telling me to stop. I thought about the consequences of drinking, especially the inability to be in the right mind. I thought about what would happen if I lost my mind because of the alcohol. I thought about being kicked out of the police academy for causing issues at the apartment complex. As a result, I poured all the cans into a sink. I cried several times, wondering about my inability to address the mental health crisis in my household. After crying, I remembered that I still had homework to do. Then I wiped my tears and prepared myself for the following day's training by completing my homework. This became my routine during the police academy.

Although various problems overloaded me—specifically, dealing with a mental health problem in my household—I managed and overcame them. It took a lot of work, energy, and patience. But the result was a victory.

Have you faced two intense problems at once? What was your reaction? You need to understand that, to overcome challenges, the benefits of what you want must outweigh the pain.

In the following paragraphs, I will explain how, regardless of the challenges in the police academy and my family, I went back to school and conquered after graduating from the police academy.

THE PHD GOAL ATTAINED AFTER THE POLICE ACADEMY

Education has always been one of my top priorities. The police academy interrupted my classes at Southern New Hampshire University (SNHU) because it required particular attention. The training was time-consuming, as well as physically, psychologically, emotionally, and academically demanding. I could have been distracted after completing the police academy and abandoned school. However, even after I graduated from the police academy, my passion for education was never quenched.

I resumed taking classes at SNHU after my police academy graduation. I graduated from SNHU in January 2018 (grade point average: 3.82, or 95.5 percent). Because I had set a new educational foundation when I decided to switch majors from chemistry (at the associate's degree level) to English (at the bachelor's degree level), it was time to shift into something I intended for a long-term career. I had already been exposed to the criminal justice system and had been dealing with criminal and civil-related matters on the streets as a police officer. I then became interested in pursuing a criminal justice education. Studying criminal justice for a master's degree was the result.

In the spring of 2018, I got admitted into Sam Houston State University (SHSU) in Texas. I began going to school there for a master's degree. I had found the school after an extensive search for an excellent criminal justice school. According to the SHSU website,[18] in 2020, *U.S. News & World Report* ranked the university number two in the United States for its online master's degree in criminal justice. In 2016 and 2017, the university was ranked number one by the same report. This led me to apply and obtain admission to the school. After successfully completing all the university's requirements for the criminal justice program, I graduated in December 2019 with a Master of Science degree in criminal justice (grade point average: 3.75, or 93.75 percent).

Figure 5.8: Master of science graduation day
In December 2019, I obtained a master of science degree in criminal justice from SHSU.
Fidele Sebahizi

---

[18] Veronica Gonzalez Hoff, "College of Criminal Justice Online Program Ranked No. 2 Nationally," Today@Sam Article, Sam Houston State University, February 7, 2020, https://www.shsu.edu/today@sam/T@S/article/2020/cj-ranking-usnwr.

The following semester, in 2020, I began a Doctor of Philosophy (Ph.D.) program in criminal justice—homeland security. Like my previous searches for better schools, I conducted a thorough examination online during the last semester at SHSU for the Ph.D. program. I preferred the online Ph.D. program at Liberty University in Virginia for several reasons. The university offered a 25 percent tuition discount to first responders and members of the military. I cherished this excellent opportunity to save money. The university's ranking was also good, and its reputation stood out. I applied and was accepted into the program. I took classes while working for the Abilene Police Department as a police officer until I graduated in May 2024 with high distinction (grade point average: 3.95, or 98.75 percent).

Figure 5.9: PhD graduation day
In May 2024, I obtained a Ph.D. with high distinction in criminal justice from Liberty University.
Fidele Sebahizi

The title of my dissertation was "Banyamulenge Immigrants' Perceptions of the Police in the United States: A Qualitative Study." I chose this topic after reading multiple research projects about immigrants' perceptions of the police in host countries, including the United States. As a police officer, I became interested in studying immigrant-specific perceptions of the police. Then, as a member of the Banyamulenge ethnic community and an immigrant myself, I wanted to examine one specific population among the Banyamulenge community: former prisoners who were imprisoned simply because of their ethnic group in the Congo during the country's Second War of 1998. The study aimed to understand the former prisoners' lived experiences with Congolese law enforcement (police officers and soldiers), their perceptions of the police in the United States, their crime reporting in the United States, and their confidence in the police in the United States.

Because I was determined not to give up on my passion for education, I found schools that allowed me to keep my job while pursuing my advanced degrees. Giving up has never been in my mind. I realized that such a mindset can take anyone very far in life.

Consider your goals and purposely choose not to give up. The results will be promising.

Below is a journal entry that guided and encouraged me not to give up on the Ph.D. degree.

A JOURNAL ENTRY THAT HELD ME ACCOUNTABLE FOR OBTAINING A PHD

In my journey, I learned one significant lesson with various steps. Determining my goals was the first step, creating plans to attain them was the second, following through with my plans was the third, and waiting for results was the final step. Of course, there were other steps in between, but these were the main ones. I wrote the journal entry below, determined to keep my promise to myself.

On July 27, 2015, after my police academy graduation, I wrote a long-term plan for my education in my journal. I was getting ready to resume my college studies. I promised myself I would abide by the diary's timeline to the best of my ability. The picture below shows the diary's title, *Amasomo* (School). The estimated year to complete the bachelor's degree in writing (English) was 2016. However, my graduation year was in 2017 (a few months off), and my bachelor's degree was in creative writing. I also estimated that I would complete my master's degree in law enforcement in 2018. However, my actual graduation year was in 2019 (a few months off), and my master's degree was in criminal justice (related to law enforcement). Finally, the estimated year to finish a doctoral degree in anything related or close to law enforcement was 2022. But I completed my Ph.D. in criminal justice in 2024. This estimate was significantly off due to numerous uncontrolled challenges I encountered. Most importantly, however, I followed through with my plan and attained the goal.

The second paragraph of the diary is vital. It states that I would complete a doctoral degree when I was forty years old and that the degree would take me at least seven years from 2015. However, it took me more than seven years to get the degree. I was forty-one when I finished my Ph.D. I also wrote in the diary that my firstborn daughter, Fifna, would be twelve years old at the time of my graduation. But she was thirteen years old—a one-year difference. Because I understood that God was in total control of my plans, I wrote at the bottom of the diary, *"Mana, nshoboza!"* or "God, support me!" Although my estimates were off, I am glad I kept my promise to myself and achieved my ambition to become a Ph.D. holder.

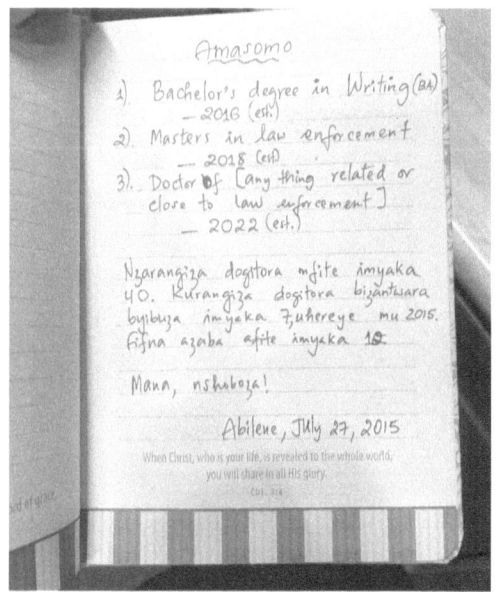

Figure 5.10: The PhD's inspirational journal entry
This journal entry became an accountability tool for obtaining my Ph.D.
Fidele Sebahizi

The journal entry helped serve the most significant purpose in my life: obtaining a most advanced college degree. That is why I preferred to include its original copy in my mother tongue here to inspire you and assure you that it could work for you because it did for me. It encouraged me to abide by my promise.

All you need is determination and consistency in pursuing your goals. It is doable when you trust yourself. Self-confidence is the key.

Chapter 6 will describe the challenges I endured and overcame as an immigrant police officer from the Democratic Republic of

Congo policing the streets of Abilene, Texas. In other words, I will discuss the struggles of patrolling American streets with my accent. However, my accent served an excellent purpose for the betterment of the Abilene community. Most importantly, you will learn about the challenges I underwent and the role my heavy but funny accent played and how it exposed me.

CHALLENGES OF AN AFRICAN BOY POLICING AMERICAN STREETS

Critics are loud, but success is louder. – Matshona Dhliwayo.

BEING A POLICE OFFICER WITH AN ACCENT

Generally, police officers encounter severe challenges while policing because of the negative reputation law enforcement has throughout the United States. But my case was unique somehow. I had to endure the general challenges of being a police officer and the struggles resulting from being seen by the general population as an outsider. My distinct accent made me stand out everywhere I went on duty. I could not get it smoother and closer to the level of a native speaker. I had to have thick skin and not worry about what people thought or said about me because the option of quitting was not an option. I chose to ignore all insults and bad words directed toward me.

This chapter reveals the universal nature of human beings. I have learned that prejudice is shared globally. It does not choose a skin color, nationality, or other type of background. The following events show what I have experienced in the United States as an immigrant police officer from Africa. As explained throughout the book, I grew up in a discriminatory world as a member of an ethnic minority group. I did not come to the United States by choice, but after surviving a historic prejudicial massacre in a United Nations refugee camp. Shockingly, regardless of its development and worldwide prestige, racial and national tendencies are still present in the United States. Sharing the following episodes demonstrates that my daily life in America relates to my early life in the Democratic Republic of Congo.

CALLED A RACIST BY A BLACK SUBJECT

The first call for service I was dispatched to during the Police Training Officer (PTO) phase as a rookie was driving while intoxicated (DWI). I was still fresh out of the academy. My PTO was sitting to my right, in the passenger seat. I was nervous because I was in the driver's seat, doing real police work for the first time. My accent also made me more anxious because I was afraid to sound different on the radio. I pushed myself through it because I did not have the choice to not communicate or to give up.

Another thing that made me nervous was the presence of my PTO, who I first thought was there to catch me making mistakes. However, he was there to help me succeed because he encouraged me, making me confident in what I was doing even with my heavy accent. At this time, I was dealing with the accent and learning how to police for the first time. I had two battles, and they both had to be won.

This first call for service was a true challenge. Reading the call sheet on the laptop, driving, paying attention to my PTO, and listening to the radio divided my attention. I had to read the call sheet to understand what I was going to deal with. It meant I had to keep up with new information from dispatch about the situation I was dispatched to handle. I still remember part of the call sheet. The driver drove recklessly and used two lanes of traffic instead of one. The driver also hit the curb, making other drivers nervous and uncomfortable. That is why a concerned citizen had dialed 911 for police help.

On my way to the call for service, my PTO asked me questions to ensure I knew what I was doing and if I was doing it right. The call sheet was updated that the drunk driver was about to park at a gas station. At this time, I was already in the area. I observed a vehicle matching the description pulling into the described gas station parking lot. The vehicle's tires were flat. While parking at the gas station behind the suspect vehicle, I transmitted a message over the radio that I was with the car at the location, providing the address: the hundred-block number and street name.

To apply the training, I turned on my police emergency lights, letting the driver know he was being stopped by the police and was not free to go. I immediately and swiftly exited the vehicle to surprise the driver. I approached the driver's side, and my PTO was on the passenger's side. The adrenaline had kicked in, and I was breathing abnormally. Now, I had several battles to conquer simultaneously and in a split second: remembering what I learned from the academy and applying it correctly, worrying about how my PTO judged my work, being concerned about my accent, and dealing with a drunk driver.

I knocked on the driver's door to instruct him to roll down his window for the investigation. "This is Officer Sebahizi with the

Abilene Police Department," I said to the driver, introducing myself and explaining why I was contacting him.

The driver had drunk so much that it appeared he was not listening to what I was telling him. I first thought his difficulty was due to my accent. It could have been. But I persisted with my interview, ignoring the accent factor. I ordered him to get out of his vehicle for Standardized Field Sobriety Tests for drunk drivers. He surprised me when he said I was racist. I was surprised because he was a Black driver, and I was a Black police officer. I could not comprehend how I could be a racist toward a Black person like myself. Was my accent a factor in his view of racism? I have asked myself several questions to this day. However, I found some possible answers that I will discuss later.

I later learned that wearing a police uniform changed my identity in some people's views. I quickly found out that I was no longer a Black man from Africa to some citizens—specifically, those who played the racism card to advance their agendas.

While labeling someone based on your social perception might be convenient, avoid it because it misrepresents your true being and how things really are. Labeling people the way they are not might change your interpersonal relations.

"YOU, NIGERIAN, GO BACK TO AFRICA!"

Labeling people when upset with them or the world is more effortless and unproductive. Labeling others and calling them names hurts them. It does not matter if these names are not bad; the connotation matters most.

On a regular patrol shift, I dealt with one subject multiple times at different locations. He was causing issues and kept doing it. He was

Hispanic. Mentioning his ethnicity is essential to the story, and I do not intend to treat him differently because of his ethnic affiliation. He was not mean to me when I contacted him the first time. During the second call, he must have been tired of me or the police in general. He was drunk, and it was necessary to deal with him because he continued to cause problems. On every occasion when I contacted him, I was with other officers, but this time I was the primary officer, meaning I was responsible for the call.

"You Nigerian!" he screamed at me, clenching his jaw and furrowing his brows. "Go back to Africa."

I had to laugh at this one. I told him nicely, smiling, that I was from Africa but not Nigeria.

"You're from Nigeria. Nigerian." He insisted and sharply turned his head away from me.

The subject must have been upset and hated that I had approached him. He might have thought I had invaded his privacy or freedom. I was doing my job and had to contact him to stop his misbehavior on behalf of the entire community. Calling me a Nigerian and asking me to go back to Africa did not upset me because I expected such treatment from people like him who did not like dealing with police officers.

When you find yourself in a conflict, consider the whole situation. What is your part in it? What can you do to ease the tension?

"YOU ARE NOT AN AMERICAN, ARE YOU? YOU ARE AFRICAN!"

Labeling can take a different direction. If calling a person a name that does not belong to them hurts, how much can it hurt if the labeler denies the person's identity or existence? Unfortunately, it happened to me on several occasions.

A resident initiated a call for service and indicated there was a Black male subject who was drunk and attacking his family members with a machete. Dispatch sent me to the location with other officers to assist. The call sheet also indicated that the subject had attempted to force his way inside the house with the machete and tried to cut someone with it.

I arrived with another officer. We contacted the subject in the alleyway behind the house. He still had a machete in his hands as he was approaching us. We ordered him to put it down. He complied. We put him in handcuffs. During the investigation and while transporting him to jail, he called me all the names anybody could think of.

"You are not American, are you? You are African," he said angrily in the patrol vehicle's back seat.

"I am proud to be African." I failed to resist his provocation.

"I know who you are." He rolled his eyes and snorted with laughter. "What's your name?" He squeezed his eyes and leaned toward me, trying to read my name tag. As he struggled to read my last name, I helped him read it, ensuring he got it right.

You understand that the subject was struggling with a mistake he was making when contacted—a dangerous behavior that could have taken a person's life, including his. But, instead of apologizing for being prevented from harming others or being harmed, he insulted me for doing my job, which protected him and his family members that day.

Have you been blamed for doing the right thing, including helping those who blamed you? Is that because some people prefer trouble to peace?

"GO BACK TO AFRICA. WHO BROUGHT YOU HERE?"

It still amazes me that I was singled out among other officers and verbally attacked for doing my police job on a regular patrol day. I expected respect, as I respected others. However, things turned out differently than I thought.

A Black male subject had a criminal trespass warning from his ex-girlfriend's residence. I use his race because it plays a significant role in the story. The resident had called the police for help removing her ex-boyfriend, who had refused to vacate the house. The calling party also wanted to pursue charges for the violation. Dispatch sent me the call as the primary officer. I had two White backup officers going with me. Again, I use the officers' race because it is crucial to the story.

When we arrived, the subject was in the garage area, eating his meal as if nothing had happened. It appeared that even the police presence did not bother him. We began talking to him, but he ignored us several times. Instead, he kept eating with his head down. Because the subject refused to leave and cooperate with us and the homeowner wished to pursue charges, I had to make an arrest. Making the arrest meant physically confronting the subject and taking him to jail because he would not cooperate. The physical confrontation was on between us and the subject, who resisted arrest. After we put handcuffs on him, he looked over his shoulder at me, baring his teeth.

"Go back to Africa. Who brought you here?"

He picked me purposely because of my accent. I just smiled back at him. It was one of a few responses I had for him.

"No. I am not going back," I added calmly.

I soon realized that I was an easy target because he knew I must have been an immigrant. Being different can be a good and a bad thing. Regardless of being picked among my colleagues, I kept my composure and performed my job professionally.

When you find yourself in such a situation, you may be tempted to act outside your normal and professional self. Keep calm. It is part of life, and you will only grow by overcoming what challenges your values.

"YOU ARE SLAVES"

Being a police officer has taught me that having patience when insulted is vital. I have been called every name in the book, including a slave—interestingly, by a subject with the same skin color as mine, which is the story I am telling you here.

One day, I was on patrol. A call for service came out, and the police needed to check a residence for a subject of interest. Three police officers responded: myself, a White officer, and another Black officer. A Black family lived in the house we were supposed to check. We knocked at the door, and a Black male subject answered. It was apparent that our presence did not please him. He began cussing at us even without knowing why we were there. He kept pacing around on his porch. He said many things to us, accusing us of harassing his family, but one phrase still stuck in my mind.

"You," he said and paused, pointing at me and my African American partner while forcing eye contact with us. "You are slaves."

He did not mention names because he did not know us personally. However, it was loud and clear that he was referring to me and my African American colleague. When we told him we were not slaves, he made a comment I do not recall about our badges, as if they were given to us to work in someone else's interests. He also said something else to set us apart from the White colleague on the call. I left that call perplexed. This time, surprisingly, I was not mistreated because of my accent but because of the color of my skin, and by someone with the same skin color.

I learned that some people see their enemies through others who have nothing to do with those enemies. In other words, wearing a police uniform made my colleague and me appear different from who we were that day. Instead of seeing us as people belonging to his racial group, the subject saw us as objects and messengers from his enemy.

Can you imagine being called that, especially by someone you think should not call you that? If you were in my shoes, how would you react?

"ARE YOU FROM ABILENE?"

One simple but powerful phrase can make someone wonder why some people react the way they do. I experienced such a moment one day when I was on patrol, ensuring the safety of my community.

I was patrolling my assigned area and driving around in my marked patrol vehicle when I noticed a truck moving forward and backward repeatedly in the middle of the roadway. The truck was not marked to indicate it belonged to a private company. I drove to the vehicle to find out what was happening and see if the driver needed help. I thought the vehicle might have been broken down. I noticed the truck was in front of a house under construction. The front yard was new and covered only in dirt. There was no grass yet. I approached and spoke with the driver, who was sitting in his seat with his left leg out. I asked him what he was doing. He said something I did not understand. So I asked him for clarification.

"Are you from Abilene?" he surprised me.

As soon as I heard this phrase, my jaw dropped. I was like, "What?" What did my question have to do with originating from Abilene? My accent had done it again. He must have been having a rough day or something. After talking to him some more, I understood what he was doing. But the surprise has never left me.

I wondered why the driver perceived me as he did. I did not take long to realize it was more likely because of my accent, though he did not tell me his reasoning. I learned that I need more patience with people who are not patient with my accent.

Be patient with people who may appear different from you. Bear with them, especially their difficulties, because we are meant to help and be kind toward each other no matter the differences.

"YOU'RE JUST LIKE THEM, AFRICAN!"

Imagine being treated or viewed differently from who you are and what you represent. It was just another day on patrol when a Black subject wished I had acted or performed my job the way he wanted me to—being on his side simply because I looked like him.

I answered a call for service shortly after my squad's daily patrol briefing. When I arrived at the scene, family members had gathered in one place, and it appeared one of them was bleeding from the back of the head. Another family member was holding the head to stop the bleeding. After investigation, it turned out that the wounded man was the aggressor. As a result, he was arrested for an offense. I assisted with the call to transport the suspect to a hospital to get him medically cleared before he went to jail. While I was putting handcuffs on him to put him in the back of my patrol vehicle for transport, he started ranting insults. He was a Black person, and his race is significant to mention because of the nature of the comments he made toward me. As professional law enforcement officers, we did not react to his insults other than explaining why he was going to jail. My accent, of course, did not fail to expose me again.

While in the back of my patrol car, he asked me to look into his face and said, "You're crooked. Black motherf*. You ain't nothing, but you are just like them. Those white motherf*. African-talking motherf*. African-smelling."

As always, I said no word in response to these insults from a crime suspect. When I finished looking into his face, I refocused and minded my business, doing my job professionally. When I finished helping with his injuries at the hospital and he was ready to go to jail, he apologized.

Sometimes, people want others to be different from what they are or represent. I learned that people want to use others for their interests regardless of the consequences to the person being asked. Although he and I had the same skin color, my job involved treating every person the same way. His apology at the end of the call, which I appreciated, informed me that he was having a bad day.

In such a situation, do not act according to what others want. In other words, please do not sacrifice your job or abandon your responsibility to treat everyone with respect, regardless of their differences.

"I NEED TO SPEAK TO A NATIVE TEXAN"

I quickly realized that I had more language difficulties handling calls for service on the telephone than in person. In today's world of advanced technology, people find it hard to trust others on the phone, especially if they have not met them in person. I think this is why some people felt uncomfortable with my accent when discussing personal matters on the phone.

One day, I responded to an advice call. I do not recall what it was about. The calling party had asked a police officer to call her cell phone to discuss a matter. The call happened to be in my assigned area, so the call was sent to me. I dialed the calling party's number. She told me what she wanted advice on. When I provided advice, she listened but sounded unsatisfied. She said she needed to speak with another officer. At that moment, I did not understand what she was complaining about. Then she called dispatch back and said, "I need to speak to a native Texan." I immediately knew my accent had done it again.

On the same note, another day, I responded to a call for service in which a citizen needed an officer to call her about a situation. A daughter had accused her mother of disturbing her by calling her several times for no apparent reason. The two lived in different cities because they did not get along. I did not encounter issues talking to the daughter. But when I spoke to the mother over the phone and provided advice, she did not believe I was a real police officer due to my accent. She called her police department, which also called my police department dispatch, to verify that I was a real police officer. I would not run into this situation if I did not have an outsider's accent. I did not bother being verified if I was a genuine police officer.

I learned I should not blame people for not being comfortable exchanging private matters with me on the telephone because of my accent. Because I dealt with scam incidents in which many scammers spoke broken English, I felt some people rejected my advice not because it was not good advice, but because they could not trust that I was a legitimate police officer.

Have you ever felt you could not be trusted because of something you had no control over? How did you respond? How would you react if you had not experienced this?

"CAN I GIVE YOU A HUNDRED DOLLARS TO LET ME GO?"

Many people tend to justify drunk people when they act foolishly. I have seen people justify their actions when they were drunk by making others believe they did not know what they were doing because they had been drunk. It is also possible that some fake their actions to look innocent and excusable. A drunk driver attempted to bribe me in this way but quickly changed his mind.

A call for service dispatched to me indicated that a vehicle was stopped in the middle of the roadway with lights on, facing the calling party's residence. When I arrived, I observed the truck parked in the street. I did not contact the driver, who had fallen asleep on the steering wheel, until my backup officer arrived. I placed my patrol vehicle a few inches in front of the suspect's vehicle to prevent him from driving it forward upon being alerted of my presence. My partner parked behind the suspect's vehicle to stop it if he attempted to move backward. I then contacted the driver. It was evident he was drunk. After finishing all the steps in investigating the driving while intoxicated (DWI) incident, I arrested him and placed him in the back seat of my patrol vehicle.

"Can I give you a hundred dollars to let me go?" he asked confidently.

"Do you know what you are trying to do?" I asked. "Do you want another charge?"

After he realized his offer would constitute a serious criminal charge, he immediately apologized. I later transported him to jail for driving while intoxicated.

Do you see that what I told the driver rang a bell in his head, indicating he could get in further trouble with the law? I wonder if my accent affected his perception and if he tried to bribe me because he viewed me as an outsider. During my career, I have learned that key words and phrases make people stop faking or change their minds for better or worse.

Have you experienced this before? How have you handled it?

FALSELY ACCUSED OF RECEIVING PAYMENT FROM ONE PARTY

My ability to speak several African languages served the Abilene Police Department and the Abilene community well. I helped the department communicate with African refugees and take reports from them. However, one challenge presented itself. I realized the victims liked me and were thankful for my assistance. Conversely, those in the wrong or who did not want my professional advice did not like or trust me.

For instance, one day, I was called to assist on a call involving an African family. A family had found out that their daughter was having an intimate relationship with her boyfriend, and this had led, according to the family, to their daughter skipping school for several days. Now it was likely that she would be withdrawn from school. The girl's family had just arrived in the United States as refugees. But the boy's family had been in the country for many years.

I dealt with the two families at least three times on different days. Initially, a family member reported that the parents wanted their girl married, but the girl did not like the idea. When I arrived at the boyfriend's residence, the girl and her family were there. I spoke with the girl's mother, who claimed that, according to her culture, whenever a girl slept with a boy, that girl automatically became the boy's wife. However, she said she wanted her daughter to go back home with her, but she also wanted the boyfriend to pay her for sleeping with her daughter. I advised her that it would be illegal because it would be considered selling her daughter into prostitution. My comment surprised and shocked her. Then I spoke with her daughter, who was inside her boyfriend's room. She refused to return home with her mother. She said she would remain at her boyfriend's house. On the other hand, the boyfriend advised me that he was not ready to marry his girlfriend. He said that they were just friends and no marriage arrangement had been made between them. Therefore, the mother was given her options in this situation. The two families stayed at the residence, discussing how to handle the matter civilly and culturally.

I responded to the same residence to deal with the same issue a few days later. I learned that the girl's family could not take their daughter home with them that night. She had decided to stay at her boyfriend's house. But this time, the girl's boyfriend called and reported that he did not want his girlfriend at his house. The girl was asked to leave because she did not live there. She refused to leave. I spoke with her family over the phone, explaining the situation and why she had to return home. They did not like my responses. They started claiming they believed the other family had paid me. I advised them it was not the case and that they could call for another police officer if they did not like how I handled the call. When I finished, I learned that the girl's family had called dispatch and accused me of receiving payment from the other family to side with them. The family may have carried the perception of the police from their native country to the United States.

I learned that refugees who needed my assistance and perceived me as helpful liked and trusted me. However, those who thought I did not serve them the way they wanted me to disliked me and complained about me, accusing me of siding with the opposing party.

While it may be easier to quickly blame and judge someone for not doing what we want or expect them to do for us, putting ourselves in others' shoes to see both sides of the conflict or misunderstanding is necessary. Try this the next time you find yourself in a similar situation and see what a difference it makes.

"YOU WORK FOR THEM"

I quickly learned that some people judged me easily based on their perceptions of the police in the United States. Racists interpreted the police uniform and the badge I wore to satisfy their judgments. That happened one day when I was told I was an agent of White coworkers who were with me.

During a regular patrol shift, a call for service came out in my assigned patrol area. The calling party reported that they had heard gunshots in the neighborhood. Multiple officers responded. The calling party also indicated that a red car was parked nearby, and they believed it was occupied. Two Black teenagers were contacted near the parked car. Initially, they were unpleasant about the contact. They acted suspiciously, and one seemed not to want to stand close to officers. He kept pacing around as if he wanted to run. I later learned he was an African immigrant. But his behavior and the false identity he provided made it appear that he did not want to identify himself as African. He provided a name that was not of African origin. He knew I was African, possibly by reading my name tag, through my accent, or through previous knowledge.

"Where are you from?" he inquired.

"Congo Kinshasa."

"I am from Congo Brazzaville."

There are two countries in Central Africa by the name of Congo: The Democratic Republic of Congo, with Kinshasa as the capital city, and the Republic of Congo, with Brazzaville as the capital city. They are next to each other.

Then the teenager began accusing me of working for my coworkers, who were all White. "You work for them," he said.

"No. I don't."

He shook his head while smiling in disagreement.

It did not make sense that he was labeling me as an agent of my White colleagues when they were the ones dealing with him and his friend. One of them was the primary officer on the call, meaning he was the leading investigator. I came after they had already made contact with the subjects. I failed to understand what made the African subject label me an agent when I was a backup officer. I learned that blame can originate from unrelated circumstances.

Do not blame people for no apparent reason. Do not use blame to justify your wrongdoing. If possible, do not blame at all, since blame does not serve a proper or constructive purpose.

"OH, AFRICAN!"

Not all people treated my accent the wrong way, and not every person I encountered diminished me because of it. Some people felt relieved when I showed up on rough days of their lives and preferred to speak with me rather than my coworkers.

One day, I responded to a call about a disturbance in progress, in which family members were fist-fighting. When I arrived with several other officers, the family was out of control in the street. Each officer was talking to one or two individuals to get their sides of the story. I approached one family member, who said, after noticing my accent, "Oh, African!" He said it cheerfully, as if he felt relieved and excited. Then he gave his side of the story.

When one of the family members was arrested on the spot during the investigation, others started complaining, including the person who had been happy to see and talk to me. Officers attempted to calm them down. An officer tried to speak to the individual I was talking to, but they did not get along. When I spoke to him again, he calmed down and listened because I had already built a good rapport with him due to my accent.

I learned that, to him, my accent set me apart from the rest of the police force on the call that day. It also helped calm him down, preventing him from causing more issues with my coworkers.

Consider your differences (what you have that others do not) an asset and a contribution toward the betterment of others. What you consider a deficiency in your life may benefit others.

"WELCOME TO ABILENE"

Just like how sober people acted differently toward me, drunk people did too. People generally behaved differently based on several reasons—primarily how I approached them and how they perceived me.

I dealt with an intoxicated person in a public place one day. He was elderly and needed to go somewhere safe because I did not think jail would help him. He had only a few teeth left in his mouth, making it difficult for me to understand him. He must have realized I was not from the United States because of my accent.

"Where are you from? Are you from England?" he mumbled.

"No. I am from Africa."

"How long have you been in Abilene."

"Since 2015."

He gave me a fist bump and said, "Welcome to Abilene."

This small, friendly conversation indicated that the older man was happy about my service—specifically, that I did not take him to jail that day, as he was aware of his intoxication. His friend stopped by later and brought him home in his vehicle.

I learned that my accent was viewed as similar to that of someone from England, though I had never been to Great Britain. I learned the English language in the United States. I liked the "Welcome to Abilene" comment. It made me feel at ease and supported.

Have you been mistaken for something unrelated to your reality? How did you react?

In the next part, I will illustrate how my expertise in African languages helped two neighbors from different backgrounds (an African immigrant and a native White resident) respect each other regardless of an incident caused by one neighbor's children.

RESOLVING A MATTER USING MY LANGUAGE SKILLS

One day, my ability to speak English and Swahili helped build respect and a good relationship between two neighbors. One neighbor was White, and the other was an African refugee. The African neighbor's children wronged the White neighbor by stealing from him. My mediation worked wonders.

A call for service came out in a patrol area assigned to someone else. The call was dispatched to me because it involved a language barrier. The calling party reported that his neighbor's children had taken his mail from his porch. He also advised that his neighbors were African Americans and spoke no English. He said he thought they were refugees.

When I arrived at the location, I contacted the calling party, a White man. He explained the incident and how his neighbor's children stole his package. He said the children were with the mailman on his porch. When the mailman left the package at the calling party's house, the neighbor's children grabbed it and ran to their house. The calling party also showed me the camera footage of the incident. He added that he saw his stolen items inside the house when he tried to contact his neighbor.

I attempted to contact the African immigrant neighbor by knocking on the front door, but nobody answered. I left, advising the calling party to call back when his neighbors returned home. He called back within an hour. This time, I contacted the neighbor and spoke with him in Swahili. He did not hesitate to agree that his children had taken the package. He said they thought the package was a gift a mailman had left them. He brought me the loose items taken out of the package. The children had broken one item.

When I informed the calling party what I had discovered, he was okay with taking the unbroken items. However, he asked for the money he had paid for the broken item. The neighbor reimbursed him, resolving the issue, which could have been criminal if the victim had decided to pursue charges against his neighbor's children. He said he understood his neighbors were refugees and did not have much.

My language skills helped me explain the African neighbor's story about what had happened and why his children did what they did, relieving the White neighbor's frustration. Since I was a police officer from Africa, the White neighbor trusted me to solve the problem, and the problem was solved peacefully, allowing the neighbors to live in harmony.

Would you have handled the situation differently if you were in the White neighbor's shoes that day? Do you think the African neighbor agreeing that his children wronged his neighbor helped the situation? How would you approach the problem if you were in his shoes?

"YOU DON'T GET HEAT IN YOUR COUNTRY. IT'S IN YOUR GENES"

During my several-year police career, I developed a thick skin that allowed me to resist insults of all kinds. It has tremendously reduced any negative impact on my life. It is one of the significant benefits

I acquired and will last many years. It is a skill I cherish every day, whether on or off duty.

While patrolling my assigned area, I received a disturbance-in-progress call. The calling party indicated that her roommate was causing a scene and had a warrant for his arrest. The roommate with a warrant was acting out, and his misbehaviors were increasing with time. He knew he had a warrant and had no chance to escape. He was also aggravated because his roommate had called the police on him. When I put handcuffs on him, he became even more agitated, claiming I was rude to him. When I placed him in the back seat of my patrol car so I could transport him to jail, his agitation worsened. He started kicking and yelling. While I was transporting him to jail, he asked for cold air in the back. So I turned on the air conditioning to the maximum. Even when I double-checked the air system in the back seat of my patrol vehicle, the air was on. He continued complaining that he was not getting any air. He must have realized I was an African immigrant because he said, "I know you don't get heat in your country. It's in your genes."

I never answered him. I continued transporting him, minding my professional business. When I got him to the jail, he revealed he was sweating for numerous reasons, including medical reasons and having taken drugs hours earlier.

While being processed at the jail, he turned to me and said, "I apologize for the way I talked to you in the car. I gotta make it right."

I thanked him for it.

I learned that people tend to feel bad about themselves after they insult others, especially if those being insulted ignore the insults and are not responsible for the misbehavior. I also understood that most people who perceived me negatively or as a threat did so because of the police uniform and the badge I wore. They did not know me personally outside my work. Their reactions were based on their views on the government or perceptions of the police. I just happened to be between them and the government they did not want to deal with or obey. I was convinced they would treat me differently if we met outside my work setting in a civilian outfit.

Do not transfer your anger to an innocent person who has nothing to do with your circumstances. Own up to your mistakes and take care of what will prevent you from making more mistakes in the future.

"I AM SURE YOU DON'T UNDERSTAND THAT WORD"

It can feel confusing and like a futile effort when you are trying to help someone who is stubborn and uncooperative when they are asked to provide the information you need to deliver the expected services. In such a situation, the person in need may feel let down, while the person helping, on the other hand, may feel overwhelmed.

While on patrol in my assigned area, I answered a call for service. A citizen had requested that the police help locate her vehicle. I contacted her at someone's business, where she had borrowed a phone to call the police.

"Where is my car?" she demanded as soon as I contacted her. She sat and threw what she had in her hands on a table. She looked at me with wide-open eyes, as if she was sure that I knew her vehicle's whereabouts.

"I don't know," I said, shrugging as if I were replying to her with another question.

"I have been needing your help all day, but you never showed up." She looked down and shook her head.

"I just read about what happened earlier. A police officer came to look for you at two different locations. You were not there."

"No, no, no, no, no." As if faking a smile, she dropped her legs to the floor from the chair bar and raised her right index finger in front of me. "Where is my car?" she persisted. "I need to find my car."

"Where is it?" I asked.

"I left it somewhere."

"I don't know then."

"No, you know." She made a quick head movement, looking away and then back at me with a fake smile. "You know where my car is. You know everything. You are a police officer."

"I wish. I wish I knew everything. Okay. Do you have information about your vehicle for a report?"

She looked down and shook her head. "That is exactly the problem. I left everything in it."

She dug into her jacket's pockets and aggressively dumped everything on the table. "You see?" she said, pointing at receipts and one-dollar bills. "That is all I have left. Where is my car?"

I almost laughed. I asked for her name and birthday so I could check the system for any record of the incident.

She gave me her personal information.

"I am sure you know where my car is." She looked at me and shook her head with another fake smile as I turned toward my patrol vehicle outside

When I went back inside to recontact her, she asked, "Where is my car?" She became louder and louder. People sitting at other tables in the bar gave each other looks as they observed my interaction with her.

I had answers that did not please her. "I did not find the incident you referred to in our system."

"Your system is wrong." She insisted that the information she provided was correct and the police system was not. She took off her leather jacket, revealing a tank top and showing old bruises. "You see? My boyfriend abused me. Police officers responded and took me to a hotel. I need to know where my car is." Her car's whereabouts concerned her more than anything else. "Can you call my boyfriend? I am sure he stole my car."

We both stepped outside. I called the boyfriend and learned that a car dealer had taken it to a mechanic for her. She used my phone to speak with her boyfriend, but their conversation was not constructive. As a result, the boyfriend hung up.

"Call him again, please," she told me while sitting on the curb, looking away from me. So I did. She spoke to him, but the conversation became more intense, and they could not understand each other. He hung up again.

"Call him again." She looked down and shook her head, covering her face as if she was about to cry.

I tried calling him and said, "I just called him, but the call went straight to voicemail. I am sure he does not want to talk to you anymore."

"No. He does. I know he's talking to someone else."

"I can't keep calling someone who doesn't want to pick up the phone, and I don't want to bother him. He has the right to refuse to answer calls from my phone."

She said something I did not catch and then looked away from me. "I am sure you won't understand that word."

That got my attention almost immediately. It reminded me that she had mentioned that I was an immigrant whose first language was not English. It also linked to a statement she had made inside when she asked me where I was from. When I replied that I was from Africa, she said, "I know, I know, I know," waving her hand in front of her as if to make me feel at ease.

"Please, call him back." She stood up and approached me and said, insistently, "I need money for a hotel. I have been outside for days without taking a shower."

I felt tired of explaining myself. I headed to my vehicle. She followed me.

My phone rang. It was a number from the state she said she was from. I remembered that her boyfriend had asked her to speak with her mother for help, but she refused.

I took the call from the unrecognized number on a speaker phone, saying, "Hello! This is Officer Sebahizi. How can I help you?"

"Mom," the woman I was with and who needed police assistance said, intercepting the call before the caller responded. I stopped and let her speak with her mother.

"Here," I handed her my phone, which was still on speaker.

"Mom, can you tell the officer to take me where my car is to get my stuff? He is upset with me."

Unfortunately, I did not take her to her car. Her request was against my department's policy.

"Okay. Thank you, officer." She handed my phone back and walked away, unhappy after refusing her mother's constructive advice.

This interaction gave me the impression that many people focus on their problems, obscuring their thoughts and failing to realize their participation in the problem-solving process. The citizen needed help understanding that her vehicle's information was essential for the investigation, including taking a report or running it in the system to get relevant information about it and its whereabouts. The failure was the result of her thinking I knew everything about her car, including its location. I also believed she was under the influence of alcohol or a type of narcotic or had blacked out because of the stress she was experiencing.

Have you ever argued with someone who withheld and could not provide relevant information about a situation but insisted on receiving your help? It can be stressful to try to help someone who withholds information you need to fix their problem.

"WHY ARE YOU HERE? WHERE ARE YOU FROM?"

It was a regular patrol shift. I was dispatched to a disturbance-in-progress call involving a pedestrian standing in the middle of the street, stopping vehicles. It was also reported that the subject was wearing a ski mask and yelling at himself. The calling party suspected that the subject had mental health issues or was high on drugs. Messing with vehicles had led to a confrontation between the subject and drivers.

When I arrived at the location, I quickly recognized the subject based on the description provided by the calling party. I turned my police emergency lights on because I had to park facing the oncoming traffic on the opposite side of the roadway to make contact. When I began engaging with him, I found him looking through businesses' doors and windows. He was holding a backpack and a basket of fruits. His demeanor changed when he realized I was behind him, and he began smiling at me. He said he was not doing what was reported to the police dispatch. I started gathering the subject's information for my documentation to conclude my investigation. He gave me his first name and spelled it. When I asked for his last name, he said it without spelling. I requested clarification, asking him to spell it out. He instead kept repeating it. Then, he said it was a name in movies.

"I don't watch movies. Please spell your last name for me." I held my notepad and pen as I waited for a response.

"What? Then why are you here?" His demeanor changed instantly, like a light switch had been pushed. He became angry, lost his calm, and began moving around. "Where are you from?"

"That is not the problem, sir. It is not the reason why I am here."

"Yes, it is."

"Why is it? I don't have to watch movies to be a cop. That is not a requirement."

"I thought you have to know literature or things like that." He slowly placed the basket of fruits on the ground as he gave me a fake smile. "Do you know me? Everybody knows me around here." He placed his backpack down as well.

"Can you spell your last name for me, please?"

"Where is your backup? Where is your backup? You better have your backup here. I am good. I am cool." He shook his shoulders up and down. He pulled his ski mask down and widened his eyes at me. "Now you know who I am? You know who I am?"

His suddenly changed behavior gave me goosebumps. I took it as a threat. I started repositioning myself, ready to defend myself if needed. He leaned down, holding his mask. When he came back up, he took the mask off and smiled widely at me. At this time, my backup arrived. Then, when I asked for his last name again, he gave it to me and spelled it out. He provided me with his date of birth as well. I let him go after checking who he was in the system.

What would be your reaction if you were in my shoes?

Working as an African immigrant police officer in the United States taught me one life lesson: prejudice is universal. During my law enforcement duty performance, I was called racial names by people from diverse races, including individuals from my own race: Black people. They did not like how they behaved, which got them in trouble. As a law enforcement officer, I did my job according to the law. As a result, they blamed me for their misbehavior and told me to return to Africa.

In short, most subjects discussed in this chapter had one thing in common: they hated the state I found them in and blamed me for things I had nothing to do with, which is a human nature.

CONCLUSION

The first life challenge I encountered was a poor beginning: growing up in a disadvantaged village with no roads, electricity, or running water. Even the toys I played with in childhood lacked comfort, convenience, and efficiency. Regardless, I enjoyed my early life because I did not know better. My life improved after I learned and accessed many advanced necessities in other countries. One simple example is learning to drive a car and owning one for daily transportation. However, I still miss many things about Africa—specifically, the community bond that united everyone in a village. Because survival required intense physical work, villagers joined one another to accomplish one task at a time before moving to someone else's task. This reciprocal system got life moving efficiently.

Unfortunately, the poor conditions I was born and grew up in followed me outside my village. In the Congolese city of Uvira, about sixteen miles west of Bujumbura, the capital city of Burundi, my parents struggled to pay the two-dollar monthly school fee for my high school education. In Bukavu, the capital city of the Congolese South Kivu province, about seventy-eight miles north of Uvira, I could not continue with my college education because of a political conflict that later turned into an ethnic-based one, which forced me to return to my family in Uvira. Here, my ethnic community, the Banyamulenge, did not have rest. Fleeing was a must.

After fleeing my country to Burundi, a neighboring country to the east, for safety due to ethnic persecution, a calamity occurred in a United Nations refugee camp, a place where we believed we would be protected. The camp had two sets of tents, and regional armed groups attacked only the Banyamulenge's set, killing and injuring hundreds. It later became evident that the camp's structural division made it easier to target and kill only the Banyamulenge refugees.

Enough was enough. I had had enough misery, and it was time to relocate to the United States as a political refugee after surviving the refugee camp massacre. The struggle for American cultural integration was enjoyable compared to previous struggles. I began pursuing the American dream in San Diego, California, by attending college.

In Abilene, Texas, the American dream became more attainable. Despite a mental health illness in my household, I refused to use it as an excuse to lay aside my goals. With a mindset of not quitting, I became the first immigrant to serve the great community of Abilene as a police officer. I also became the first member of my ethnic group, the Banyamulenge, to serve the American community as a police officer in the United States. While performing law enforcement duties, I earned a bachelor's degree in creative writing, a master's degree in criminal justice, and a PhD in criminal justice—homeland security. To quote the Bible, I did everything through Christ, who strengthened me. However, I faced challenges as a police officer. I endured racial slurs from a few citizens I arrested or dealt with for breaking the law. After serving the city of Abilene for more than seven years now, despite the prejudice I experience from angry citizens, I look forward to striving for more challenging personal and professional achievements. I teach and encourage my thirteen-year-old and six-year-old daughters to always aim high in their lives and be willing and ready to face challenges rather than avoid them.

Sharing my story has been a relieving method of releasing and unloading confined, uneasy memories. It's a way of letting go of the past, like taking a deep breath. It's something that needs to be done repeatedly. Sharing my story assures me that people who listen to me, as human beings like myself, will be obligated to be sympathetic toward me. Even sharing my story with an indifferent person gives me some relief. Sometimes, it feels like a moral obligation to share my story, good or bad, with others to help them grow.

What about you? How do you feel when you tell someone about something that bothers you internally? What about a good memory you don't want to keep to yourself?

ACKNOWLEDGMENTS

Thanks be to the Almighty God, the Creator of the universe and humanity, for protecting and empowering me. Without Him, this book would not be available.

I thank my parents for always being there for me regardless of struggles and challenges.

I thank all my teachers from elementary to Ph.D. for investing their knowledge in me.

I thank everyone who assisted in gathering information to accomplish this work.

Though I could not locate the photographers or sources of some pictures in the book, both the original and illustrated photos, I am thankful for them wherever they may be.

ABOUT THE AUTHOR

Dr. Fidele Sebahizi grew up in a poor African village, living and surviving an ethnically-motivated massacre in a United Nations refugee camp of Gatumba in Burundi, Africa. Fidele overcame life obstacles as an immigrant in the United States to achieve the American dream. He became the first immigrant to join and work for the Abilene Police Department in Texas as a police officer and the first member of his ethnic group, the Banyamulenge, in the United States to serve the American community in such a capacity. While working for the APD, Fidele earned multiple degrees: a B.A. in Creative Writing from Southern New Hampshire University in New Hampshire, an M.S. in Criminal Justice from Sam Houston State University in Texas, and a Ph.D. in Criminal Justice—Homeland Security from Liberty University in Virginia.

A father and a husband, Fidele likes to listen to country music during his free time.